EUROPE
IN THE BALANCE

SECURING THE PEACE
WON IN THE COLD WAR

CHRISTOPH BERTRAM

A CARNEGIE ENDOWMENT BOOK

©1995 by the
Carnegie Endowment for International Peace
2400 N Street, N.W.
Washington, D.C. 20037
Tel.(202) 862-7900
Fax.(202) 862-2610

Europe in the Balance may be ordered from Carnegie's distributor,
The Brookings Institution, Department 029, Washington, DC 20042-0029, USA
Tel. toll-free in the U.S. (except Washington, D.C.): 1-800-275-1447;
in D.C., call (202) 797-6258. Fax (202) 797-6004.

Photo: AP/Wide World Photos.
Design: Paddy McLaughlin, Concepts & Design.
Printed by Automated Graphic Systems.

Library of Congress Cataloging-in-Publication Data

Bertram, Christoph, 1937-
Europe in the balance : securing the peace won in the cold war / Christoph Bertram.
120 pp.   cm
ISBN 0-87003-068-X
1. Europe—Politics and government—1989- 2. North Atlantic Treaty Organization.
3. European federation. 4. Europe—Strategic aspects. 5. Peace.
1. Title
D2009.B47 1995
327. 1'7'09409049—dc2O   95-35108
                                                                          CIP

CONTENTS

PREFACE

Almost six years after the walls came down in Europe and almost four years after the Soviet Union disappeared into history, how to assure the peace that was won in the Cold War is, or should be, the dominant theme of Western political debate.

To some extent, that debate is taking place. But it is all too often conducted in separate, even isolated compartments. Those who advocate enlarging the North Atlantic Treaty Organization (NATO) rarely focus on the internal problems of an alliance that has lost its chief enemy. Those who concentrate on political and economic integration within Europe seem to take for granted the Atlantic connection that has been central to both the security and the integration of Western Europe. And although there is much discussion of how to promote reforms and stability in Eastern Europe, strangely little is heard on the future role of Russia in the affairs of the continent. Rarely, if ever, are all of the elements analyzed together that must be addressed together to secure the peace won in the Cold War.

This book owes its existence to my frustration over the one-dimensional approach so widely practiced, as well as to the opportunity provided me by the Carnegie Endowment for International Peace to do something about this gap. For half a year, from January to June 1995, on a leave of absence from the German weekly *Die Zeit,* I had the chance to do what I had criticized others for failing to do, namely, to examine the various elements and institutions required for future European stability and the ways they will have to complement each other. The following pages are the product of these six months.

This essay makes no claim to be the definitive work on the future of European stability. Its ambition is to broaden and sharpen the debate; its concern is that without such an effort, the decisions that the West's political leaders have to take in the near future may fall short of what is required. This is not a book of footnotes but of reasoned opinion; I have tried to do justice to counterarguments, but I have not shied away from stating my conclusions forcefully. While I hope, of course, to convince my readers of these conclusions, I shall be grateful if those whom I fail to convince at least feel that they, too, have to reexamine their positions.

I could not have written this essay in a more congenial environment. The Carnegie Endowment provided me with all necessary facilities as well as with kind and stimulating colleagues; Moises Naim was a constant source of cheerful, yet probing, criticism; Morton Abramowitz and Paul Balaran, president and vice-president of the Endowment, respectively, were both demanding and encouraging reviewers; my research assistant Doug Johnson was a patient and helpful sparring partner. A study group of knowledgeable and thoughtful people from government and academia, chaired by Barry Blechman, met several times while the book was in progress, sharpening my thinking whether they agreed (which they sometimes did) or disagreed (which they did often) with my analysis and conclusions. Jonathan Davidson and Gregory Treverton kindly reviewed the manuscript and helped me avoid mistakes of fact and thought; those that remain are my own.

I am indebted to all for the time they gave to this project as well as for their engagement in lively, enjoyable intellectual exchanges on an issue central to the future of Europe and the West. My hope for them as for all others is that, when they read this book, they will not feel that their time was wasted.

Finally, my thanks go to my wife Ragnhild and our children Rebecca, Mathias, Jakob, and Caroline for joining me in this American adventure and thus making it possible. I hope that when they look back upon these six months, they too will feel that it was worth their while.

September 1995
Washington, D.C./ Hamburg   Christoph Bertram

FOREWORD

by Lawrence S. Eagleburger

Just as the French Revolution shaped much of the nineteenth century and the Russian Revolution much of the twentieth, so will the end of the Cold War and the collapse of the Soviet Union cast their shadow over at least the early decades of the twenty-first century. Violent change in France and later in Russia fundamentally changed the rules of both national and international politics. It remains to be seen how much will change in the aftermath of the peaceful revolution we have so recently witnessed.

Nineteenth and twentieth century history is largely the story of how Europe (and later, the United States) adapted to the changes wrought in France and Russia; how well, in other words, European and American leaders were able to build a "new world order" from the ruins—and opportunities—of revolution. One can, I suppose, argue the merits of the Congress of Vienna and the Treaty of Versailles, but history tells us that neither was much more than an attempt to hang on to as much of the past as possible. And to the extent that Versailles sought to create a "new order" in Central Europe, it was manifestly a failure.

But we do, sometimes, learn from past mistakes. An historically unprecedented set of wise and creative statesmen, following the close of World War II, did set out to bring stability and prosperity to a devastated Europe. Their accomplishments were of historic proportion in both political and military terms. An aggressive Soviet Union was kept at bay, while the Europe to its west was rebuilt and the roots of democracy were put firmly in place.

There is no need, here, to detail that success, except to emphasize that it was the result of institution building on a grand scale: NATO, the OECD, the IMF/IBRD, the European Union in its various stages, etc.

Those who were "present at the creation," as Dean Acheson entitled it, had lived through two world wars and were determined that past mistakes would not be repeated. Those experiences, plus the growing threat of Soviet aggression, were the cement that held the West together as it built its own new world order.

Now, some fifty years later, we must ask whether we will be the victims of our own success. The collapse of the USSR, we thought, would put an end to the division of Europe. Instead, we see old divisions—old national hatreds—taking center stage from the earlier East-West divide. We see increasing questioning (particularly from the younger generations) of the permanence and importance of the trans-Atlantic relationship. And we more and more hear and see national leaders unsure of how to deal with the consequences of the revolution we created and so long sacrificed to achieve.

Christoph Bertram, in this volume, provides us with eminently sensible answers.

First, don't just sit there! Do something! The structure we have built so successfully is being questioned—sometimes for good reason. To wait until we have a "clearer" vision of how to proceed is to assure that things will get worse.

Second, what is needed is refinement of already existing structures, not a wholly new "architecture." We do not have to repeat the miracle of the immediate postwar years. But we do need to modernize, adjust, and adapt institutions to our new realities.

But let me not, here, repeat what Bertram says so well in the following pages. His arguments are insightful, his recommendations compelling.

EUROPE IN THE BALANCE

INTRODUCTION:
EUROPE IN THE BALANCE

Today, Europe is the defining region for the future of international affairs, and the next few years will be decisive in this respect. This does not mean it is more dynamic than Asia, or more relevant than America. It merely means that events in Europe and the way they are handled during the remainder of the twentieth century will have a profound impact far beyond the continent itself.

If for the first ninety years of this century Europe was at the center of international politics, this was mostly for negative reasons: European power rivalries produced World War I; European domestic upheavals led to a Hitler and to World War II; and during the Cold War, European conflict had the potential to trigger nuclear armageddon.

When the Cold War came to its unexpected and unexpectedly sudden end in 1989, many in and outside Europe rejoiced that the age of Eurocentrism was finally over. If Europe remains at the center of international affairs nevertheless, this is no longer due to the dangers that European instability can still generate but to the example that Russia, the United States, and Europe will set in dealing with the problems of the new Europe.

The dangers cannot, of course, be discounted. For the past four years, Europe has been the scene of a murderous Balkan War that only now shows signs of ending. The disappearance of communist repression has revealed old ethnic tensions in the former Soviet empire that in the past often were the fuses igniting wider European conflict and that now are heightened by the social strains that accompany the change from state to market economies. The disappearance of Soviet control not only allowed German reunification but also elevated Germany to the status of Europe's major power; the country's past, however, remains a source of suspicion and anxiety among its neighbors. The new states that emerged from the ruins of the Soviet Union weakened Russia but also created new flashpoints of military conflict and temptations for Russian intervention. The collapse of the old walls freed Eastern Europe but also opened Western Europe to the problems as well as to the populations of that region. Immigration has become an explosive social issue in

1

many Western European societies. Europe after the Cold War is clearly not a continent of peace and harmony, and it could be a continent of foreboding. Yet, as the Balkan War has demonstrated, what tensions, dangers, even wars occur are generally contained regionally—in contrast to the situation during the Cold War years, when they would have had immediate global consequences.

Today, precisely how the major powers act in and toward Europe, and how they respond to developments there, will have a decisive impact on international politics. It is primarily in Europe, not in Asia, that Russia's overall international role will be tested and shaped. It is the links to Europe, not to Latin America or the Pacific rim, that will determine whether the United States remains actively involved in the maintenance of international order. And it is in Europe that the fate of the most successful and promising international institutions ever established for the peaceful cooperation among states—NATO and the European Union—will be decided. If these fail here, constructive multilateralism everywhere will lose its best models.

If Europe is where the international role of Russia will be decided, it is of course largely due to geography: Russia is predominantly a European power, even more so now that its ability for worldwide reach has been severely curtailed. The nature of Russia's links with its European neighbors will be the most important factor in shaping its international image, signaling not just to the region, but to the rest of the world as well, the sort of power Russia wishes to become.

This will apply both to Russia's policies in its immediate vicinity and to its dealings with countries and organizations further west. A Russian strategy of deliberate destabilization vis-à-vis, say, Ukraine or Georgia would be seen abroad as proof of a neo-imperialist renaissance in Moscow. A Russian policy of pressure and great-power threats against Poland or the Baltic republics would raise alarm throughout and beyond the continent over a new "Russian threat." In fact, unless Russia demonstrates that it can live peacefully with its neighbors, its claims of having outgrown imperialist tendencies and become a reliable and constructive member of the international community will be unconvincing.

It is not vicinity alone, however, that makes Russia's behavior in Europe the test of its future overall international role. Europe is also the world's region with the most closely knit network of multilateral organizations through which states have become accustomed to formulate, develop, and conduct a large portion of their foreign policies. Russia is not used to such multilateral procedures; its history has not prepared it for working within them, and its yearning for status—even more touchy now that its power has so visibly declined—makes it difficult if not impossible to integrate Russia into the major existing institutions. Yet trying to keep Russia outside this framework of policy consultation, coordination, and compromise would only strengthen its sense of isolation and heighten the temptation to define Russia's interests in a way irreconcilable with those of its neighbors. One of the major strategic tasks of the West is to offer Russia a place in the multilateral European framework; for Russia, a major strategic test for its European and international future is whether it accepts, and how it operates within, such a framework.

For the United States as well, the relationship with Europe will be the litmus test of its future world role. Europe is the main, if not the only, anchor tying the United States to extra-hemispheric international order. The anchor may not hold. Americans may become tired of a Europe absorbed with its own identity but continuing to need the involvement and perhaps the deterrent of the United States to prosper in peace. But if that happens, the United States will be saying farewell not only to Europe but to international commitments as well.

The reasons for this are both cultural and institutional. Historically, the United States is more familiar and comfortable with Western Europe than with any other region, and if it is not willing to stay tied to Europe, it may not be willing to maintain ties anywhere. In addition, the United States has a unique institutional involvement in the affairs of Europe. It maintains bilateral security treaties with countries all over the world and has armed forces stationed in many of them. But the only multilateral institution that holds U.S. foreign policy to a procedure of day-to-day consultation and coordination with other sovereign states is the North Atlantic Treaty Organization that links Europe and North America.

If this link were to break, either because NATO faded away or because Americans grew tired of their commitment, U.S. international involvement would become essentially unilateral. Commitments would be entered into and reneged upon at will, with freedom of maneuver becoming the ultimate objective of U.S. foreign relations. This would not mean an end to U.S. interventions in international affairs. But it would amount to the abdication of any sustained, predictable, and reliable U.S. commitment to international order.

The future of Europe, too, will be decided in Europe. This is less obvious than it may sound; after all, for decades the fate of Europe was determined largely by two superpowers—one of which, the United States, was situated across the Atlantic and the other, the Soviet Union, lay on the periphery of Europe. Today, Russia is politically peripheral to the fate of Europe, and the United States, although still central as a balancing and assuring element in European politics, largely leaves to Europe the definition of the future structure of the continent.

Yet the map on which that structure should be charted has lost the clear contours imprinted by five decades of division. This is obvious in the case of Central and Eastern Europe, where the change has been dramatic. It is no less significant in Western Europe, where the changes have been gradual but no less far-reaching.

Because of the measured pace of developments in Western Europe, there has been a tendency to assume that somehow only the East, not the West, would be in for a massive redefinition. This was clearly an illusion. Today, the decline in the United States' leading role and the increase in Germany's political as well as economic weight drive the reassessment in the minds of European politicians and deeply affect the future of the European Union (EU), the dominant post-World War II model for the continent's future. Will the new circumstances now encourage re-nationalization over integration? Will the driving force of European integration, the Franco-German entente, break up as France finds its German partner too big for comfort? Will Europe's smaller countries now fear domination and marginalization by the larger ones, and in response encourage rivalries and divisions all too familiar to European history?

Finally, it is in Europe that the future of multilateralism will be defined. Europe has been, and will remain, the testing ground for multilateralism—that is, for the readiness and ability of modern states to subject their relationship to each other as well as their policies to a common procedure and common oversight. Like no other part of the world, Europe has spawned a panoply of international organizations to address issues of common concern. These organizations are today the most imaginative legacies of the Cold War: NATO, institutionalizing the United States' commitment to Europe's security; the European Union, pooling the sovereignty of its members; the Organization for Security and Cooperation in Europe (OSCE, the former CSCE), helpful in the "soft landing" of the Soviet Union's collapse and now instrumental in defusing the potential for ethnic conflict that emerged in its wake; the West European Union (WEU), the long-dormant framework for European defense coordination; the Organisation for Economic Co-operation and Development (OECD), the chief body for economic consultation among industrial states, including North America, Europe, and Japan; and the Council of Europe, the cultural and human rights organization—to name but the most significant.

Among these institutions, two stand out: the NATO alliance and the European Union. Over four decades, they together helped to make Western Europe stable, prosperous, and safe. They have set, for countries elsewhere in the world desirous of establishing resilient structures of regional cooperation, a model for successful interdependence.

NATO institutionalized coalition defense for Western Europe and succeeded in a feat never performed before or since: bringing the United States into a formal multilateral security relationship with Western Europe. The vague commitment of the NATO treaty—that allies would regard an attack against one of them as an attack against all and assist each other by such action as they "deem necessary"—hardened into a nuclear guarantee, into tight military integration and close-knit political coordination.

The European Union (until 1993, the European Community) went even further by creating a covenant among its members to pool national sovereignties; to remove national borders in other than their geographic content; and to legislate, increasingly by majority decisions, for the Union as whole.

Yet both NATO and the EU today find themselves in a state of anxious uncertainty. For NATO, this is caused by the loss of the enemy, the old Soviet Union, that had justified its existence. Can this extraordinary alliance find a new purpose in the new international circumstances, or has it lost its function and will it soon loose its cohesion as well? Can it be retained as a military insurance policy against new dangers, whatever these may be?

For the European Union, uncertainty results from growing doubts among European citizens and governments about the wisdom of transferring further powers to the Union and from the danger that its original supranational objective will be diluted by the inclusion of more, and increasingly more diverse, countries in north, south, east, and central Europe. The promise that the EU could become the major framework for prosperity and stability for Europe as a whole thus contains the risk that cohesion will be lost by further enlargement, opening the way to the old, unsettling rivalries and competing coalitions for which Europe was known, feared, and despised. For all of these reasons, Europe is the region where the international image of Russia, the international commitment of the United States, and the future of the major multilateral institutions of the West will be defined.

Act Now—or Wait and See?

There are those who dispute the need to take any action now and advocate temporizing instead. Perhaps not surprisingly, this approach is well represented in current Western governments. The direction in which Russia will develop, the temporizers argue, is by no means clear; NATO, although eventually requiring reform, can go on as it has for a few more years; in the European Union, difficulties have always been resolved in compromise; and the United States, while preoccupied with internal concerns, still remains fundamentally disposed toward maintaining strong ties to Europe. In contrast to the Cold War years, when the inherent risk of nuclear war imposed the need for rapid action, the West can now afford the luxury of "waiting and seeing"; there is no need to rush to conclusions and decisions now about these central and complex issues.

This argument is tempting but not persuasive. Waiting for certainty means forgoing influence; passivity means that things will fall into place by accident rather than by choice. This approach also underestimates the costs of ambiguity.

How long does the West want to wait before working out a formal, stable relationship with Russia? Already a Western policy that is half-cooperation in case Russia reforms, half-deterrence in case it becomes threatening again is injecting increasing suspicion into the relationship. Many Russians appear to be convinced that the West pursues the destruction of their country under the guise of half-hearted support.

How long can NATO maintain its credibility as a military alliance when the first serious challenge in post-Cold War Europe, the Balkan conflict, has found it indecisive and wavering for years before it lately mustered the will to intervene? How long can the Alliance—after declaring that it is relevant for all of Europe—delay the decision to allow some Eastern European states to become full members of the organization? And if NATO continues to lose credibility, will not the trans-Atlantic link between the United States and Europe also decay unless it is underpinned by new efforts and cooperative institutions?

How long can the EU pretend that it can both invite Eastern European countries into its midst and, at the same time, streamline its internal decision-making? It is precisely the prospect of enlargement that imposes the need for clarity about the political purpose and the institutional arrangements of the Union; without such clarification, a community of states that set out to become a politically cohesive international actor could end up as little more than a trade area.

These are some of the reasons why a "wait and see" stance is counterproductive. Indeed, it is not as if the temporizing strategy had not been tried. To fend off membership applications from other European countries, the EU invented the time-gaining device of Association Agreements—only to discover that they increased rather than reduced the pressure to open the Union to new members. To avoid defining its relationship to Russia and the new Eastern European democracies, NATO invented the Partnership for Peace program; it is now discovering that Russia's hostility to NATO's eastward extension has hardened—as has Eastern European insistence on admission to the Western security club. In the Balkans, NATO temporized to avoid being sucked into the conflict—only to discover that it was increasingly drawn into it, if not with military forces then with its prestige, authority, credibility, and cohesion.

This does not mean, of course, that the only sensible policy for Western governments is to rush into decisions. But it does mean that temporizing is not necessarily the wisest counsel for the West in preparing the Europe of tomorrow. In this context, waiting and seeing amounts to waiting for chances to be lost rather than for options to be gained. It could be corrosive to wait until the fog of uncertainty has lifted. After all, it is in times of uncertainty that leaders can best influence the flow of events.

The next few years will determine whether NATO and the European Union can adjust to the new challenges. But much more is at stake than the fate of NATO and the EU. The future of Europe itself is involved, depending as it does on the framework these organizations form together. Indeed, it is difficult to imagine a vibrant European Union in the absence of a vibrant NATO. No less involved is whether the United States will remain internationally engaged in a structured manner. Without U.S. participation, there can be no NATO; without NATO, the United States will cease to be a power in Europe and perhaps even a reliable international partner elsewhere in the world. Finally, the future role of Russia is at stake: a failing NATO and a disintegrating European Union would leave few barriers in place to douse temptations of the old power game for a country whose political maturity will be measured by its ability to participate constructively in an orderly international process.

This essay examines the challenges and the opportunities that present themselves in this defining phase of the post-Cold War period, as Europe's future hangs in the balance. Chapter 1 looks at the special role that institutions, particularly NATO and the EU, will need to play in that context. Chapter 2 discusses the future of NATO as a military alliance. Chapters 3 and 4 examine the consequences of NATO's accepting a more political role in relation to Russia and Eastern Europe, respectively. Chapters 5 and 6 deal with the EU's prospects for overcoming its internal divisions and extending its framework of prosperity to Eastern Europe. Chapter 7 considers the interrelationship of NATO and the EU in the new Europe. Chapter 8 suggests ways to assure the continued involvement of the United States in the affairs of Europe. A concluding chapter summarizes the major findings and proposals.

It has become fashionable in the Western debate to refer to these issues as "European security architecture." That term is energetically avoided throughout these pages. Architecture connotes starting from scratch with a blueprint, a "present at the creation" exercise in which everything can be designed anew. But Europe is not terra nova; it is a very old settlement, with many old features obscured by the Cold War now reemerging and some institutions created in the Cold War still around.

What can sensibly be done is to strengthen the foundation here and there, repair and replace worn-out and faulty sections, free clogged-up drains, and add new space. It is, in other words, a task of modernization, renovation, and renewal rather than of "architecture." The most promising approach will not consist of drafting new blueprints but of adjusting, updating, and possibly extending the structures created in the almost five decades when Europe's history was frozen. That will be difficult enough. It will require luck, effort, and a strong dose of statesmanship to get there at all.

Chapter 1
COPING WITH UNCERTAINTY

Europe is a continent in the grip of enormous change. For forty years, Soviet control suppressed change; nuclear deterrence, as Raymond Aron wrote, froze history. Then, in a few dramatic months in 1989–90, the walls collapsed, communist regimes folded, and old power structures evaporated as new ones evolved. Suddenly, the old certainty was replaced by new uncertainties.

Six years later, the eruption is over, but the lava is still flowing. The changes are Europe-wide, simultaneous, and interactive. In most instances, they are healthy, but they also come up against old structures, old biases, and old privileges—creating friction, tension, even conflict. At the same time, the old barrier to Eastern European conflict, communist repression, no longer exists, and the main Cold War barrier to international conflict, nuclear deterrence, has lost its threat. In the absence of the old Cold War barriers to conflict, domestic, regional, and international tensions can now boil up into a dangerous brew.

The strategic task in Europe will be to ensure that this multitude of changes can proceed in orderly, peaceful fashion. The end-product of this process is still unclear, and will be so for a long time. Thus it is even more urgent to establish or, where they already exist, to protect and adapt, procedures that can contribute to reforms without breeding revolution or tensions that might escalate into conflict or, as in the Balkans, into war.

Dangers and Responses

While it is easy to draw up lists of possible dangers to European stability today, the exercise is essentially meaningless. Take, for example, the traditional and (among Western Cassandras) still favorite potential source of European conflict: Russia. Russian forces have withdrawn behind Russian borders, now shorter than at any time in the past 250 years. Russia may well in the end manage the transition to a stable political and productive economic system; its progress has already defied many a Cassandra. It is clearly in the interest of the West that Russia succeed, but it will be decades, not just a few years, before the matter can be judged. It will be longer still before Russia (if it is so inclined) can rebuild a power base permitting it to threaten the rest of the continent. Even among former Soviet republics—the "near abroad" dear to Russian nationalists—Moscow wields influence not primarily because of its overwhelming military power or expansionist ambitions but because of these countries' continued economic dependence on Russia.

For the foreseeable future, the security problem that Russia poses is therefore that of its own instability—the instability of government and social order, the fragility of state cohesion and authority, the brittleness of political control over the military and of physical control over nuclear and other weapons.

It makes little sense for the West to base its Eastern policy on the assumption that Russia's power, rather than its impotence, constitutes a security problem for the rest of the continent. Instead, it makes sense to think of maintaining, extending, or establishing mechanisms for orderly change in which Russia can participate and which can help to reduce the repercussions of Russian instability while underpinning those elements of stability that are emerging within the Russian Federation.

If Russia does not pose a major problem for European stability, does a united, powerful Germany perhaps do so? That question is on the minds of at least some of Germany's neighbors. It is important to remember, however, that two structural deficits—the lack of resilient institutions for Germany's domestic stability and for its international integration—contributed heavily to why that big country in the center of Europe repeatedly caused European conflict during this century. Today, with German democracy firmly established (significantly, the extension of democratic procedures and institutions to East Germany has been the most immediate and unequivocal success of unification to date), and with the country welded by treaty, recent history, and temperament into the international structures of the West, it seems farfetched if not absurd to consider Germany a potential source for future European conflict.

Germany's commitment to Western structures is firmly rooted. The lessons Germans learned from their recent history have left a deep, probably enduring mark on the country's political consciousness, instilling in political leaders and citizens alike a conviction that, at all costs, Germany must avoid isolation. This abhorrence of aloneness will continue to assure steadfast German support for strong multilateral structures just as it will make any German government in the foreseeable future give priority to working with others rather than to acting on its own.

The only conceivable circumstance under which German power in Europe might again turn into resented and resisted dominance, reenergize the search for compensating alliances, rekindle German fears of encirclement, and arouse the other usual suspects of past European power conflict would be the unraveling of the multilateral structures in which Germany and the rest of Europe have found harmony. Once again, the maintenance and refurbishment of institutions such as NATO and the European Union offers the best recipe for preventing an old problem of European instability from haunting the continent again.

Is the real danger, then, one of peripheral conflicts—in the Balkans, or in Georgia, or Algeria, for example—spilling over into Western Europe? It could well be. But nobody can be certain of cause, effect, or remedy. Even the long and bitter fighting in the Balkans has remained remarkably contained in that region. The chief security impact of that conflict on Western Europe has been indirect—pushing close to a million refugees into Western Europe, undermining the credibility of the Western Alliance, and creating the awesome precedent that, in the middle of Europe, military force is, once again, profitable for territorial gain.

But who can predict whether the precedent will be repeated elsewhere? The most likely candidates for Balkan-type strife—some of the new Central and Eastern European democracies and Soviet successor states not yet out of reach of economic and political upheavals—are displaying a remarkable degree of consolidation. They are dealing responsibly with issues related to ethnic minorities, albeit sometimes with the assistance of gentle persuasion from the West. In contrast to predictions fashionable among Western experts only a few years ago, the countries released from Soviet control have so far managed their transition remarkably well.

This encouraging state of affairs of course may not last. But if it does, it is probably due at least in part to an institutional perspective: the hope of many of these countries that they will, sooner or later, find a home in the organizations of the West, the EU and NATO. They know that this prospect will vanish if they engage in ethnic conflict or in border disputes with their neighbors. The chance of joining the Western clubs and having to qualify for membership thus increases their determination to avoid those kinds of conflicts.

It does not automatically follow that their wish to join should be granted; that discussion is taken up below. Nor does it mean that only through an extension of hitherto Western structures of order will the ability of these countries to cope with internal or trans-border instabilities be enhanced. Indeed, readier access to Western markets and Western funds could greatly ease the painful social and political surgery these countries are undergoing. In addition, however, they will need a sense of belonging, of not being out on a limb in an uncertain environment. Here again, it is the existence or absence of efficient European structures of order that will have the decisive impact on whether or not potential conflict issues flare up or remain under control.

Stability through Stabilizing Institutions

This brief sketch of conflict scenarios makes clear that the most promising approach to meeting the challenge of stable change in Europe is not to focus on any specific contingency but to maintain or establish institutions and procedures that can encourage orderly change. This is admittedly a traditional European perspective. Americans, with the good fortune of being the overwhelming power on an island continent, are less inclined to think in terms of structures and institutions tying states to multilateral procedures. Their instinct is toward solving specific problems rather than toward creating institutions to reduce the likelihood of vague difficulties becoming disruptive.

Yet the European bias for institutions is not wishful thinking. It rests on the experience that in Europe institutions have worked. Of course, they only do so to the extent that powerful states make use of them. But the fact that these states have done so throughout the Cold War may help to explain why this period of protracted East-West tension ended not with a bang but with a whimper. As Robert Keohane and Stanley Hoffmann pointed out in discussing the dying years of the Cold War: "How governments reacted . . . was profoundly conditioned by the existence of international institutions. Europe was an institutionally dense environment in which the expectations of states' leaders were shaped by the rules and practices of institutions, and in which they routinely responded to initiatives from international organizations, as well as using those organizations for their own purpose" (Keohane, Nye, and Hoffman, *After the Cold War—International Institutions and State Strategies in Europe, 1989–1991*, Harvard, 1993). Not just European governments, but the Soviet Union and the United States as well, made use of this institutional network. Indeed, U.S. involvement in NATO and the Conference on Security and Cooperation in Europe was an important element in the transition to the democratization of Europe and the unification of Germany.

The institutions that sprouted during the Cold War and assisted its demise are even more relevant to European stability today. This follows largely from the nature of the new security situation. The dangers confronting Europe today are less specific than during the Cold War, whether they concern nuclear proliferation, mass immigration, Islamic fundamentalism, ethnic cleansing, or a cut-off from energy sources. None are inevitable or automatic. The Balkan tragedy, the first major European war of the new era, is a case in point: the war was not the preordained outcome of the dissolution of Tito's Yugoslavia but the result of a combination of policy failures, none of which by itself would have triggered the conflict.

During the decades of East-West stand-off, the space between ominous signs and conflict was tight; the moment Soviet tanks moved across a tripwire, war would start and escalation would be unleashed. Today, the space between disturbing events and conflict is wide. There is no tripwire anymore. When faced with warnings of impending crises, governments understandably feel little urgency to act—who knows, perhaps the danger will pass, their leaders are advised by political and military experts.

One factor that does have a predictable influence on whether the potential becomes acute, however, is the existence or the absence of international institutions sufficiently powerful to prevent the combination of factors that turns tension to conflict and conflict to war. Of course, international organizations will only take action if their member governments are willing to make use of them. But through the procedures they establish, they make it easier for governments to act; this is both less risky and less demanding than starting from scratch.

Just imagine if Yugoslavia had been a full member of the European Community (or even just an aspiring candidate) in 1990, the year before its various republics opted for independence and stumbled into war. They would then have been involved in a procedure designed to reconcile national independence with regional interdependence, turning the sights of political leaders to economic prosperity for their people rather than to territorial conquest and "ethnic cleansing." The burning fuse would have had a better chance of being extinguished before it reached the dynamite. In the tight space of immediate threats, institutions can rarely intervene effectively. In the wider space of indirect contingencies, they come into their own.

The other reason why international institutions have a greater role to play in Europe after the Cold War than during it is that they can serve as guide rails through uncertainty. When the threats to security and stability are vague and the relationship between states is in flux, when there is no clear coordinating system of power and priority, international institutions and procedures allow governments to hedge against the surprises of uncertainty.

That is why, contrary to the predictions of the so-called "realist" school of international relations, NATO did not collapse along with the enemy it had been designed to deter. Similarly, it is not surprising that public support for this alliance in many of its member countries is as high, if not higher, today than during the Cold War. States, just as individuals, seek reassurance in times of uncertainty, and international institutions often provide a measure of reassurance for them.

In times of certainty, institutions mirror the realities of power. In times of uncertainty, they can shape the realities of power. During such times, states are likely to be more willing to tie their hands because, by tying those of others, they not only reduce uncertainty but also gamble that they might get more out of the bargain than they have to put in. Bargaining is easier when the currency is not yet fixed. Since signatories to international institutions lose some freedom of maneuver, the fact that they cannot fully calculate that loss in times of international uncertainty makes the sacrifice more acceptable.

The uncertainties of European change suggest that an institutional response is needed. Specific threats are not the problem, and contingencies cannot even be pinned down. It is the health of European structures of order that will determine whether a simmering problem becomes a threat. That is the decisive factor—whether one worries about a diminished Russia, a resurgent Germany, or the instabilities of social and national development spreading from East to West or from South to North. If no institutions to channel change existed, they would have to be invented. European stability is to a very great degree defined by the stability of European institutions.

The Alliance and the Union

Fortunately, the two most extraordinary international organizations created after Word War II, NATO and the EU, are still in place. Unfortunately, they cover only the Western part of the continent, and both are entering a precarious period as their purpose and cohesion are strained in the new post-Cold War world. This raises some basic questions for the future of European stability: Can these organizations adjust to the needs of a Europe that includes not only the countries of the Western part of the continent? Can they retain their cohesion in the process? And what, if any, complementary institutional arrangements are required?

Some may argue that to limit this examination to NATO and the EU represents an arbitrary choice. Other institutions, such as the Council of Europe, the oldest European institution, and the Organization for Security and Cooperation in Europe (OSCE) have the advantages of being less identified with the era of East-West deterrence than NATO and more flexible than the supranational EU, with its comprehensive ambition and its cumbersome decision-making machinery. Both the Council and the OSCE, moreover, have shown that they can make useful contributions to the promotion of the rule of law and to ethnic detente in Eastern Europe and the former Soviet republics. The OSCE, in particular, has been helpful in reducing tensions with the Russian minority in the Baltic states and may provide other mediating services elsewhere on the former territory of the Soviet Union.

It does not diminish these two bodies to recognize, however, that they are and will remain secondary to the task of assuring orderly change in Europe. The Council of Europe has always seen itself as an expression of European values and rules, assisting the efforts of organizations with executive power but not aspiring to take their place. The OSCE is still more the Conference it used to be called rather than an implementing body; it also suffers from the defect of most traditional intergovernmental institutions: it can decide only by consensus, and its membership is so large (over 50 states) that consensus on any serious issue is nearly impossible.

This fundamental shortcoming has rightly discouraged all those who, not least in Moscow, for a while considered making the OSCE the major European security organization, endowed with a Directing Council and supervisory rights over other security-related international bodies in Europe, particularly NATO. It is inconceivable that NATO countries would agree to such subordination. But even if they did, the OSCE as an intergovernmental body can only agree on the lowest common denominator, and since its membership is so diverse, that denominator will always be very low and the organization will be paralyzed in any real controversy.

NATO and the EU are very different from the Council and the OSCE in their substantive concerns as well as in their decision-making. Formally, NATO, like the OSCE, is a purely intergovernmental organization in which consensus is the condition for agreement, and every member state has a veto. But the shared purpose of the organization (to protect its members against a major present threat), its limited number of signatories, and the undisputed leadership of the United States facilitated and maintained consensus to such a degree that members accepted a measure of military integration that practically committed them to full participation in the common defense.

This cohesion, which gave NATO authority in the past, has, not surprisingly, weakened with the end of the Cold War. But it is still orders of magnitude stronger in NATO than in any other European institution apart from the EU. The machinery facilitating agreement among members is still in place. Moreover, NATO has committed the United States to Europe in a way no other institution could. To a large degree, this was due to the fact that the United States regarded a threat to Europe as a threat to itself. But even today, when that unifying threat has gone, the tradition of U.S. leadership assures a major, often decisive role for the United States in NATO.

Whether NATO can maintain cohesion, authority, and U.S. involvement in Europe is thus the crucial question for the ability of this alliance to both continue to function as a military reassurance against future dangers and serve as a framework for stability for the wider Europe. Will the disappearance of a Soviet Union, the decline in U.S. leadership, or the possible enlargement toward Eastern Europe deprive NATO of its unique features and let it decay into a traditional intergovernmental organization?

The EU owes its cohesion not to an external enemy or an external leader but to a shared objective and an unprecedented legislative process designed to limit the veto power of its member states. That shared objective was and perhaps still is the progressive integration of national policies into a common European entity, starting with economic matters. And although the legislative process leaves the right to decide to the states, it gives the prerogative to propose to a supranational Commission; many decisions do not need the approval of all to be binding for all.

Whether the Union can continue to function effectively and become relevant to European stability in general will depend on the ability of its members to coalesce around its basic objective and to assure that national vetoes cannot block its progress. This ability is under a cloud of doubt today, since both the ultimate aim and the method of integration have become matters of dispute within the Union. If both were lost and the EU degenerated into little more than an intergovernmental free-trade arrangement linked to an agricultural subsidy fund, it would cease to provide a framework of stability for Western Europe. The EU would also fail to qualify as a protective structure for the wider Europe that keeps the dangers of instability at bay and enhances the prospect that change can occur without disorder.

As structures of order for the continent, NATO and the EU are the only serious candidates. Together, these two organizations have been central to Western security and prosperity; if their adjustment is successful, they will be equally central to ensuring orderly and peaceful change in the wider Europe. Their state and prospects, their difficulties, and their ability to overcome them are therefore the main focus of this essay. Both institutions are in difficulties today whether they do or do not admit new members. Both have to redefine what they are about. For both, the resilience of the trans-Atlantic relationship will remain a determining factor. This is obvious for NATO, which by definition will fall apart if the United States cancels its involvement. It is true as well for the European Union, which without the underpinning offered through NATO could easily drift apart in intra-European quarrels and suspicions.

Chapter 2
ALLIANCE WITHOUT A CAUSE?

Like old soldiers, alliances whose task is done just fade away. History is replete with military pacts that fell apart after the dangers that brought them about had vanished. Can the NATO alliance, now approaching fifty, evade a similar fate?

For over two generations, NATO has succeeded in integrating the military practices and security policies of sovereign states. It gave credibility to the incredible—that the United States would be willing to respond with nuclear weapons to any attack on an ally far away, on the other side of the Atlantic. Most extraordinary, perhaps, the NATO alliance succeeded in protecting all its members for over forty years without ever firing a shot in anger.

Nor did this organization collapse when the threat of Soviet power had gone. An alliance created to protect its members against attack not only accomplished its mission but then also helped to manage successfully the messy and potentially dangerous transition out of the Cold War into an unknown peace. It allayed Soviet and Eastern European concerns over the reunification of Germany. It offered a framework of dialogue and recognition to the newly independent republics of the former Soviet Union and the old, once again independent countries of the former Warsaw Pact. Today, it is seen by many of these states as the only security club they want to join—as quickly as possible.

Yet past success does not in itself justify future existence. Is it worth the effort to keep alive an alliance that has done its duty and to try to adapt it to the very different post-Cold War world? Would it not be both more honest and politically sensible to disband NATO and, in its stead, set up a new security organization not associated with the tensions, crises, and security requirements of decades past?

Perhaps there was such a rare and brief moment between the unification of Germany in October 1990 and the collapse of the Soviet Union in December 1991, when leaders in the East and West felt confident enough and bold enough to play with the idea of a new, Europe-wide security arrangement of sufficient authority and cohesion. But if that moment ever existed, it is no longer open today. To disband NATO now would throw Europe into deep insecurity. It would cut the only multilateral link between the United States and Western Europe. It could fuel tensions between Russia and some of the former Soviet republics, such as the Baltic states. It would threaten political stability in the newly democratic states of Eastern Europe and political cohesion among the integrated states of Western Europe. For both Europe and the United States, it would be a strategic disaster.

The alternative suggested by some—replacing NATO with a European security organization, backed by a U.S. security guarantee against the invasion of Western Europe—is not a realistic option. A European security organization without full U.S. participation would lack credibility in the eyes of many, if not most, states within and outside Europe. That the United States would be willing to give a security guarantee to a Europe that pretends to be able to do without it is highly doubtful; that it would do so without the degree and kind of control that NATO's political and military integration provides is practically excluded. The suggestion to replace NATO thus amounts to disbanding it without putting a credible alternative in its place.

Hence the question is not whether NATO should survive but whether it can survive, not whether it ought to have a future but what its future can be. If it is difficult to provide a confident answer, this is because the crisis of NATO is complex and serious and cannot be overcome without a major reorientation.

NATO's Existential Crisis

As old NATO hands are fond of pointing out, the Atlantic Alliance has weathered a good many crises, from Suez in the 1950s to Vietnam in the 1970s and European missile modernization in the 1980s, to name but a few of the more outstanding ones. Indeed, they like to remind one, crisis has been the normal state of affairs in this organization of independent and sometimes jealously sovereign countries. And yet the consequence they draw from this record, namely that NATO's new crisis is no more serious than those of the past and should therefore not be exaggerated, is fundamentally flawed.

In all previous NATO upheavals, one element remained central: Soviet power and ambition threatened all members equally or was at least perceived to do so. This threat overshadowed all other considerations; it "militarized" international as well as trans-Atlantic relations by giving priority to common security concerns, and these concerns in turn generated the discipline needed to overcome whatever divisions arose among members. The perceived threat from the Soviet Union inevitably reunited the Atlantic Alliance.

The new threats are different: They are divisive, not unifying; they are cumulative rather than immediate; and they are coalition-breaking, not coalition-forming. In the past, the big danger again and again jolted NATO's sixteen nations into common assessment and common action. The new, lesser dangers produce sixteen different assessments and sixteen different reasons for inaction.

The Balkan War is typical of the new condition, not (as many claim) a special case. It exemplifies the new kinds of dangers Europe is confronting. It demonstrates the difficulty for NATO of mustering, for most of the duration of the conflict, more than the unity of inaction. Only when, after over four years of war, the costs of inaction became too high did the Alliance coalesce around a plan to bring an end to the fighting. NATO member states were incapable of grasping early on the strategic significance of the conflict. And their hope of finding a new role for their alliance as the military arm of the United Nations or the OSCE proved illusory.

In the Cold War years, fighting in Yugoslavia would have sent alarm bells ringing immediately all over the West. Many a "World War III" scenario originated in an assumed Balkan crisis following Tito's death; in these scenarios, the Soviet Union would not hesitate to exploit the situation in order to expand its zone of control, and the West would scramble to counter the Soviet threat. The conflict would have had the highest strategic significance for the Atlantic Alliance as a whole.

Now it is much more difficult to recognize a strategic crisis when it occurs. When the Balkan War started in the summer of 1991, Western governments were unanimous in their view that the issue was of marginal concern to their security. Despite all the talk of the need to broaden the definition of security, leaders smugly stuck to the oldest, narrowest definition: that a threat to security is a military threat to national frontiers.

Western leaders not only were blind to the risks of the conflict widening or escalating; they did not even understand until much later that the war would undermine the credibility of an alliance that claimed to be the only functioning security organization in and for Europe. And while the instinct of Western politicians and their military experts was to stay out, they and the NATO alliance were instead drawn deeper into the conflict without being able to control it. Bosnia became a quagmire for the West (the favorite argument of Western officials for staying out!) not least because of Western willingness to let others dictate the course of events. It was only when, in the Fall of 1995, the balance of military advantage was shifting away from the Bosnian Serbs to the Croat and the Bosnian governments that Western powers, under U.S. leadership, finally took events in their own hands, for the first time adding a major military punch to their hitherto wavering diplomacy.

Those who want to categorize the Balkan War and NATO's performance in it as an exception, a maverick event from which no general lessons can be drawn, have to explain in what way future threats will be different from this one. If anything, the new dangers to Western security will be even more indirect than in the Balkan case. They will not involve direct challenges to Western borders through invading armies and tanks but indirect ones arising from the prospect of mass refugee movements. They will not threaten the survival but the cohesion, confidence, and authority of the West. They will not destroy the center but destabilize the periphery of the Alliance's security area. They will no longer entail the risk that the world will be blown up in a nuclear holocaust but, if unopposed, they will encourage those contemplating military force for political or territorial gain. Can anyone who claims that Yugoslavia is a special case argue with confidence that NATO members will behave differently when the next such conflict erupts?

All other conceivable conflicts will be further afield—whether it is ethnic strife in Southeast Europe, tribal wars in the Caucasus, Islamic revolutions shaking Northern Africa, or a new Gulf emergency. The fact that the West was unable to regard the European Balkan conflict as a common threat suggests that it is even less likely to respond multilaterally to most of these other eventualities. This non-response could occur not only in conflicts outside NATO territory, but even within it; if, for example, Turkey were drawn into regional conflict as a result of the Kurdish crisis, its NATO partners would not readily come to its assistance.

It was at least in part to acquire the capability to deal with these new types of conflict that NATO developed the concept of "interlocking institutions," defining for itself a new "out of area" task within the network of international bodies trying to cope with conflict and disorder: If NATO members so decided, the military arm of the Alliance, the most powerful enforcement instrument in the world, would be at the disposal of the United Nations or the OSCE.

But even during the Cold War, when conflicts beyond NATO's territory were often perceived as part of East-West rivalry, NATO alliance members could never muster a concerted "out-of-area" effort; even then these conflicts proved divisive. Now that they are no longer seen as elements of a global competition but as regional or even local events, the idea that NATO would find new cohesion in "out of area" operations impresses by its naivete. In addition, the concept has practical flaws highlighted by the way in which NATO became involved and entrapped in the Balkan War.

The first flaw lay in the illusion, often encouraged by governments and usually popularized by the media, that organizations like the United Nations or the OSCE can act on their own volition. They are of course purely intergovernmental bodies, with no life of their own except that breathed into them by the states that are their members and masters. Delegating tasks between "interlocking institutions" thus amounts to NATO nations holding as many vetoes against doing anything as there are organizations in which they are represented, e.g., NATO's Council, the U.N. Security Council, and the OSCE. They can block in one what they have supported in the other and use inability to agree in each as an alibi for doing little or nothing at all. The relative success story of the Gulf War only proves this point: the anti-Iraq coalition prevailed not because the United Nations functioned so well but because the states taking part in it agreed among themselves on what to do.

The second flaw was to pretend that NATO, when lending its military arm to another organization, would still remain in control. What happened was the reverse: the operative rules ceased to be those of NATO and became those of an umbrella organization with a very different agenda. Superficially, this facilitated agreement in NATO; thus the consent of all sixteen governments to impose the United Nations' no-flight resolution over Bosnia or to conduct airstrikes for the protection of U.N. forces was possible not least because the governments most opposed to military intervention, particularly the United Kingdom, could rely on the determination of U.N. commanders on the ground to avoid any serious action. In substance, however, it exposed NATO's inability to agree on a common strategy in the conflict and only underlined its weakness: NATO, the world's most powerful multilateral military organization, could only act under the control of the world's least forceful organization, the United Nations. An alliance whose credibility lies in its ability to use force consented to becoming the servant of an intergovernmental body whose credibility rests upon its impartiality as a negotiator.

This suggests that NATO's inability to take timely joint action, as displayed in the Balkans, is now not the exception but the rule: faced with the new types of indirect dangers that are most likely, the Alliance will be united only in the determination to do nothing; every project for common action as opposed to common inaction will be highly divisive. It is not true that Western governments were deeply divided over what to do in the Balkans; they were united by the firm desire to do nothing serious about the war—a basic consensus often obscured by disagreements over secondary points.

It is true that, in the late summer of 1995, over four years into the Balkan War, the Alliance finally seemed to rediscover the determination for decisive action. NATO aircraft conducted a major campaign against Bosnian Serb positions in order to push their leaders to agree to a compromise plan, and Alliance governments insisted that the NATO force pledged to watch over the implementation of a peace accord would be under NATO operational command, authorized but not commanded by the United Nations. Yet while these events were helpful, perhaps even decisive, in bringing the Bosnian War to an end, any claim that they showed a Western alliance that had finally developed a realistic formula for future "out-of-area" operations fails to convince.

None of the NATO actions suggest the Alliance's determination or ability to address jointly, and in a timely fashion, the conflicts of the future. What they do suggest is that Western governments, having allowed themselves, by their own half-heartedness, to be drawn into the conflict, will in the end try to disentangle themselves from it. Even then they are unlikely to engage in forceful military intervention; significantly, NATO's willingness to dispatch some 50,000 men to Bosnia-Herzegovina at the end of 1995 was contingent on the cessation of hostilities there. Hence NATO's overall record in the Balkan conflict, its more impressive military investment toward the end included, confirms the systemic difficulty it faces in mounting "out-of-area" operations. The new dangers are still divisive, not unifying, and the Western alliance is ill-equipped for meeting them.

Nor can American leadership, as some have argued and still hope, regenerate the old sense of common purpose among allies. It is, unfortunately, the nature of the new kinds of indirect dangers that they lack the message of urgency and the prospect of dire consequences that give determination to the leader and discipline to the followers. Leadership can do a lot; but even if the United States were willing to exercise leadership, it could not inject into the new dangers the unifying impact of the old threat.

Of course, it is still possible, if unlikely, that one distant day a new Russia might loom threatening over the European continent. But alliances come together under the impact of a present and common threat. As long as the threat remains at least plausible, they can even hibernate during periods of peace. The vague possibility of a major danger forming in a far-away future will not, however, provide sufficient glue. Those who count on some kind of Zhirinovsky-led Russia filling a forlorn NATO with a new sense of purpose are victims of self-delusion: even if Russia should fall under the control of ultra-nationalists, its economy would still be weak, its army in serious straits, its internal strains enormous, and its ability to shape events in Europe marginal. Instead of regaining their old cohesion, NATO countries would react no differently than they have to other non-immediate dangers—by disagreeing about the severity of the event, the response it requires, and the timing of an eventual response. They would agree only to procrastinate.

The old NATO no longer exists because the threat that held it together no longer exists. A new NATO cannot be developed as an "out of area" military subcontractor to other institutions because its members cannot be counted upon to stand together in any "out of area" crisis. What then can keep this alliance alive?

The Minimalist Approach: Clout in Reserve

One answer might be: Retain NATO as a military asset to be held in reserve for uncertain contingencies not only in Europe, but in the Middle East, the Gulf, and elsewhere.

This minimalist concept has its attractions. It does not require a new raison d'être for the organization but concentrates on the most tangible aspects of forty years of Atlantic military cooperation and integration. It does not require that a new enemy be defined. It retains the Alliance as a useful consultative arrangement for foreign and security policies and for maintaining common military assets that might one day become relevant again.

The minimalist approach is not overly concerned with the problem that, in future crises and conflicts, the members of the Alliance may fail to stand united. Who knows—perhaps they will. And even if not everyone did agree on common action in a crisis, some allies might still form "coalitions of the willing" and make use of NATO's joint assets with the acquiescence of the rest. The model for such coalitions is the 1990–91 Gulf War, during which NATO supplies, communications, and procedures were employed although neither the Alliance as such nor all of its members were involved.

This minimalist approach also provides a rationale for the continued deployment of U.S. forces in Europe; it offers bases for troops and pre-positioned equipment should the United States wish to dispatch forces to conflict areas more conveniently reached from Europe than from North America. It appeals to defense planners in Europe and the United States at a time of tight defense budgets: Why write off the unique assets of infrastructure and integration that NATO has built up over the years? It does not open up a potentially divisive debate over the future of the Alliance. And it lends a consistent argument against extending NATO eastward: Why include countries that contribute little in military assets but much in political complications? Moreover, is it not also in the security interest of the new democracies of Central and Eastern Europe that NATO's military capability remain effective and undiluted? Thus the minimalist option avoids the two most difficult questions that a reassessment of NATO would raise: how to assure the continued involvement of the United States in the security of Europe and how to adjust the Alliance to the changed strategic situation on the continent.

Appealing as it might appear, the minimalist approach has a major defect. It assumes that NATO's political cohesion and military organization will remain largely unchanged and that an "Alliance in Reserve" can hold together without a common threat and without a clear prospect that it will be used, and used effectively.

The Strains of Change

NATO's military organization already shows the strains of change. With the disciplining justification of the Soviet threat gone, the Alliance has to accept much greater flexibility in its operations—less consensus and more ad hoc arrangements. This is already the case, as noted above, in the political assessment of, and the reaction to, some of the new dangers. It also applies, however, to what has rightly been regarded as the unique feature of this alliance: namely, military integration.

The unraveling of military integration is taking place; it is even explicitly accepted. The January 1994 NATO Summit gave its official blessing to the West European Union (WEU), that fledgling body in which Western European countries claim to develop a defense identity of their own, to employ NATO resources in crises that the wider alliance does not recognize as its own. Regardless of whether the WEU will be able to muster that degree of cohesion (Chapter 7 argues that it is unlikely to do so), the Summit decision is a significant departure from the previous principle of integration.

NATO's integration used to be based on the key idea that, since an attack against one member would be an attack against all, military personnel from all member states should serve in its staffs; France's 1967 withdrawal from the integrated military command was regarded as a sinful aberration. Now, Combined Joint Task Forces are to be set up and made available for subgroups within the Alliance willing to use them; "coalitions of the willing" are envisaged as the most likely model for the future, formed ad hoc and composed not necessarily just of member states but also of countries outside NATO. The Alliance's ambitious motto "e pluribus unum," forming a whole out of many parts, is being replaced de facto by "ex uno pluria," i.e, creating many parts out of the whole.

Integrated procedures are being replaced by ad hoc arrangements negotiated according to circumstances. In the decades of deterrence, the procedures through which NATO commanders requested forces from member governments were designed to assure immediate response.

Today, such requests are subordinated to political scrutiny and supervision at each step of the way. When in November 1994 NATO's Supreme Allied Commander in Europe (SACEUR), following formerly agreed procedures and after informal consultations, requested six reconnaissance aircraft from the German Air Force to serve over Bosnia, he ran into major and unexpected difficulties. Not only did the German Government, given its small parliamentary majority, regard the request as politically inopportune; Bonn also found support from NATO's Secretary-General and from Permanent Representatives on the NATO Council who felt that the authority to decide such a move now had to lie with them, not with the military. Willy Claes, then Secretary-General, even publicly disavowed NATO's top military commander by declaring that the request to Bonn had been only an unofficial exploration. When asked why he had done so, the former Belgian Foreign Minister replied (in an interview given to the author in December 1994): "Because I have a long experience with conducting policy in coalition governments."

It was an apt comment on the new working conditions in the post-Cold War Alliance. While NATO has always been based on the need to get political approval from member governments, that approval could always be assumed likely. Now, previously agreed procedures are being replaced by detailed, case-by-case political bargaining, and coalitions must be sewn together for every new contingency.

This may be regrettable, but it is inevitable. The growing incursion of national political considerations into NATO's operational procedures is merely the logical consequence of a strategic situation in which no security crisis affects all NATO members in the same way at the same time and in which actions being considered are no longer motivated by a fear for survival. The integration of military planning and staff work, a major factor in NATO's past accomplishments (and for all those who participated in it, a matter of considerable pride), has been loosened.

No longer are all the nations represented in NATO staffs willing to take part in all operations. Member states also no longer commit themselves unquestioningly; they may even withdraw their forces from a joint operation because they change their minds—as the United States did in November 1994, when it withdrew its ships from the naval force policing the U.N. weapons embargo against former Yugoslavia. Imagine the United States unilaterally withdrawing its armies from the Fulda Gap (a region through which Soviet tanks were expected to advance in case of war) during the Cold War!

Flexibility in coalitions, in procedures, and in integration will become normal for NATO. It will also extend to what few in the Alliance dare yet admit: flexibility of commitment.

Significantly, the central commitment of the North Atlantic Treaty is defined in much looser terms than is generally assumed. It is useful to recall the wording of the central article of the Treaty, Article V: "The parties agree that an armed attack against one or more of them in Europe or North America shall be considered an attack against them all, and consequently agree that, if such an armed attack occurs, each of them . . . will assist the party or parties so attacked by taking forthwith, individually and in concert with the other parties, such action as it deems necessary, including the use of armed force, to restore and maintain the security of the North Atlantic area." There is nothing here of automatic military assistance or of standing by a partner in need with all the means at one's disposal. And those looking for a reference to a "nuclear guarantee" will search the Treaty in vain.

What made assistance practically automatic, including the nuclear means of the United States and the United Kingdom, and imposed tight operational procedures, were the requirements of Cold War deterrence. To defy possible Soviet plans or to dissuade Soviet temptations to attack the West, a force had to be organized that would be capable of immediate response and would have escalation credibility. These requirements no longer exist, and they are not likely to be in demand for a long time. The removal of NATO's primary enemy and primary purpose has made assistance no longer automatic and has deprived the "nuclear guarantee" of its erstwhile operational meaning.

Attempting to carry over the concepts evolved under a unifying threat into the new period of diverse and disuniting dangers is bound to meet with failure. Just as the old reality imposed its interpretation on the Treaty, so will the new realities, triggering allied support for an attacked Treaty partner not when it is simply in trouble but perhaps only if it is in dire straits. This does not mean that the Alliance should now formally renounce the interpretation of the Treaty commitment as practiced in the era of East-West deterrence. But it does mean accepting that, unless those special conditions return, relations among NATO members and within the organization will be flexible, less predictable, and more cumbersome.

NATO is becoming more of an ordinary alliance because the circumstances of European security are no longer exceptional. The idea that this organization can somehow be frozen in its past state of military integration, to be defrosted in an emergency, is highly unrealistic. This is a major flaw of the "minimalist" approach.

Moreover, the approach is essentially technocratic, not political. The Alliance's military tasks are drying up; cases in which it will muster consensus for immediate joint action will be rare. There may be some cases when subgroups, coalitions of a few willing governments, may come together to address a particular crisis. But these, too, will be few and far between, and instances in which the other, passive members will consent to grant a minority the use of their joint assets will be even rarer. There is no sense in pretending otherwise: The military functions that remain cannot substitute for the purpose NATO lost when the West won the Cold War. Military reassurance will remain welcome; the potential for joint military action, even if seldom activated, will remain desirable. But the Alliance will not survive as a military organization; nor can the military organization survive unless the Alliance itself finds a common purpose beyond that of merely keeping military assets in reserve.

The New Mission: Securing the Peace After the Cold War

But how should a new common purpose be defined? It is óne thing to list the advantages that accrue from NATO's existence and quite another to articulate convincingly what would tie the Alliance's members together in future. The advantages of NATO's continued existence are obvious: by assuring the political presence and involvement of the United States in the affairs of the European continent, NATO makes German power tolerable for Western Europe and living in Russia's shadow bearable for Eastern Europe; it sustains Russian interests in developing cooperative relations with the West as a whole; and it discourages temptations to ethnic strife in Eastern Europe.

These obvious benefits from continuing the Alliance will not, however, suffice to give cohesion to the Western club. The reason why more is required lies partly in the need of democratic societies to justify their international commitments by aims superior to the advantages inherent in the existence of these commitments. It lies, too, in the nature of politics: politicians do not just want to administer, they want to present achievements and get credit for them. If NATO could be run as a bureaucratic exercise only, shielded from public debate, the undoubted advantages that its existence represents might just be enough to hold it together for a bit longer.

But this choice does not exist. Moreover, it would be a doubtful one. Only a vibrant alliance can assure continued U.S. involvement in Europe. As a largely logistical operation that administers dwindling military assets for a phlegmatic membership, NATO would soon lose its balancing and stabilizing potential. It would also over time lose its ability to function as a modern military organization if the need should arise again. Like old soldiers, it would be condemned to fade away.

To maintain their alliance, NATO members cannot afford the "minimalist" approach. Instead, for NATO's sake, member states have to formulate and pursue a more ambitious common project that is sufficiently appealing to its peoples and attractive to its political leaders. The most obvious and promising one is also one that Western politicians have instinctively, if often imperfectly, embraced over the past few years: to turn NATO into a "network of reassurance"—a framework of stability extending beyond the present membership—for the continent as a whole. Will this project be both captivating and unifying enough to breathe new life into an old alliance? A number of indicators suggest that it may be.

First, Western statesmen are conscious of the historic challenge with which the end of the Cold War has presented them. They know that peace cannot be assured by making only Western Europe secure— Eastern Europe must be included as well, since its fate is now intertwined with that of Western Europe. Stability in what was once the Soviet empire will define stability on the continent.

Second, NATO's as yet cautious steps toward playing the role of continental reassurer have enjoyed public support on both sides of the Atlantic as well as a growing consensus among allied governments. If anything, this has been due to the sense that here was an obvious, natural task for the West to address. This vague unanimity may vanish once NATO governments have to take concrete decisions. They have not yet devised an agreed strategy for turning the Alliance into a wider network of reassurance, nor have they seen eye to eye on the steps needed to reach that goal.

Whether, when, and how many new members should be admitted to the Atlantic Alliance is still an open question; parliamentary majorities for ratifying the NATO accession of, say, Poland have not been secured; and how the future relationship to Russia should be constructed is still an open issue. The debate on these matters will, quite rightly, be controversial. Yet looking back over the years since the collapse of Soviet control in Eastern Europe, the measure of Alliance consensus that NATO's stabilizing impact must not stop at NATO's borders is impressive.

Finally, the notion that winning the peace after the Cold War requires willingness to rethink and possibly expand Western institutions has had particular appeal in the country that matters most: the United States. With the disappearance of the direct threat that linked the fate of Europe to that of the United States, the European theater quite naturally is diminishing in U.S. strategic planning; new technologies favoring the rapid deployment of military forces from the continental United States further reduce dependence on European bases. For these reasons, NATO is no longer as important to U.S. military requirements as before. Hence it is of considerable importance that another common goal be identified that can engage the United States in the Alliance.

No common project that does not also engage the United States will serve to keep NATO together. Perhaps surprisingly, the task of underpinning peaceful change on the continent of Europe seems to have done so. It is natural for Western Europeans to be aware of the impact of Eastern European instabilities (although, as the Balkan War testifies, they have been good at looking the other way) and to think of addressing them. It is not as obvious why Americans would wish to be involved in this task.

Yet despite the decline in bipartisanship in U.S. foreign policy and an obvious inward-turning trend in the country, a sense of responsibility for the fate of Eastern Europe—even the possible extension of NATO membership to some of the new democracies there—still seems to enjoy bipartisan support. This support may turn out to be rather soft once the tough questions of NATO extension have to be asked and answered. Will the U.S. Senate agree to a treaty stipulating that an attack on Hungary or Poland, for example, should be regarded as an attack on the United States, possibly involving U.S. forces and even a U.S. "nuclear guarantee"? Will the United States reconsider once Russia responds to NATO extension plans by freezing the pending U.S.-Russian arms control agenda, as Russian representatives have already warned? That is, of course, possible. Already, the U.S. foreign policy establishment, in contrast to the Administration and Congress, is voicing growing opposition to NATO's eastward expansion. The positive attitude of the public to date may change when the political and material costs the United States would have to pay for a more intensive involvement in stabilizing Eastern Europe are defined.

The main point, however, is that the United States seems to be in favor of such an involvement. Washington, after all, has taken all the major initiatives to articulate NATO's role in this stabilization process, often against initial European resistance. The Partnership for Peace— the program designed to promote practical cooperation between NATO staffs and the new or newly democratic countries of Eastern and Central Europe, including Russia and the other member countries of the Commonwealth of Independent States—was conceived by the Clinton Administration. Similarly, NATO's current efforts to define the conditions of membership before entering into formal negotiations with candidate countries would not have been made without Washington's prompting. As discussed below, this does not mean these were necessarily the right steps to take. It does mean, however, that the United States is engaged in making NATO relevant for European stability as a whole. If there is any common project for the future of the Western Alliance that can enjoy widespread American support and even solicit U.S. leadership, this is it.

To sum up: NATO remains essential for stability and security in Europe. But the military tasks it can reasonably be expected to perform are unlikely to endow it with a sufficient raison d'être. For its own sake, to assure its own survival, the Alliance has to devote itself to a new common project. None is more obvious or accepted, and none enjoys more U.S. support than that of providing a network of reassurance not just to Western Europe, but beyond.

It is unfortunate that much of the Western debate on this subject has focused on only one of its aspects: the opening of NATO's membership to the states situated between Russia and the West. This is obviously one, but only one, logical consequence of NATO broadening its tasks from making the West secure to stabilizing a continent. If the Alliance were willing and able to project its military power beyond its borders, the issue would be less clear-cut. But if it is true, as has been argued earlier in this chapter, that NATO is unlikely to be able to do much to provide security "out of area," extending security and stability through extending its membership follows naturally. This not only protects those inside against (unlikely) aggression from outside; it also can help to defuse tensions within, just as NATO has helped prevent a Greek-Turkish war despite deep antagonisms between these two Alliance members, or has helped former enemies to become partners in the European Union.

Yet NATO enlargement can be only one of several tools that the strategy of establishing a network of reassurance for all of Europe requires. If the Atlantic Alliance wants to live up to the historic challenge presented by the end of Europe's Cold War division, it must try to offer to Western Europe, to Russia, and to Russia's European neighbors a framework in which they can all feel secure. How this might be done in relation to what must be the central consideration in any eastward stabilization policy by the West, namely to Russia, is the subject of the next chapter.

Chapter 3

RUSSIA AND THE NEW NATO

If NATO countries want to do their part to extend the existing Western European structures of stability to the whole continent, they must start with the question of how to fit Russia into these structures. Amazingly, and unfortunately, Western policy, after an initial phase of wavering, has not seriously addressed that question. Instead, the debate has focused on the smaller and much less problematic countries of Eastern Europe, as if European stability could be achieved by bypassing the largest state on the continent.

NATO's new focus on all of the European continent rather than the Western part alone has been discussed and advanced primarily as a matter of extending NATO membership to the new democracies of Eastern Europe. Many of those who favor NATO's enlargement do so with a potentially dangerous Russia in mind; many of those who oppose it do so in order not to antagonize Russia. But neither group seems to have given much thought to what the future European role of Russia should be and what kind of relationship the West should establish with that country.

So far, NATO countries have offered Russia a Partnership for Peace arrangement but, apart from recent proposals for more frequent consultation, little more. When Moscow, as foreseeable, objected to the admission of some Eastern European countries into the Alliance, the only response of Western leaders seemed to be to seek to overcome Russian opposition, not to address the central question of Russia's place in the new Europe. And yet, this question—so important for the future of European stability—needs to be addressed.

What Kind of Russia?

However much NATO has changed from the Cold War days, however sincere the intention of its member states that the new task of the Alliance be political rather than military, its most visible operational expression continues to be in the form of soldiers, weapons, and military staffs. The military is the currency in which NATO deals; indeed, if it were otherwise, it could not aspire to the stabilizing role it now has to play. Hence NATO expansion closer to Russia's borders must appear threatening to Russian nationalists; to Russian moderates, it must appear as a move to exclude Russia from equal participation in European affairs.

It is therefore either thoughtless or dishonest to declare, as the West is doing, that NATO enlargement is inevitable and Russia need not worry about it. As a considered policy, this makes sense only if the West expects the main successor state of the Soviet Union to become, within a few years, either irrelevant or a deliberate spoiler of stability and security in Europe. In the former case, Russia's reactions do not matter; in the latter, the strategic consequences are obvious: Western defenses have to be improved against a resurgent Russia by turning much of what in the Cold War years was the security glacis, the forward defense zone of the Soviet Union, into the security glacis of the West. That is indeed what some (although not all) of the Eastern European aspirants to NATO membership are claiming and what some (although not all) of those in the West favoring NATO expansion are arguing—that the Western Alliance must extend eastward to contain a Russia that sooner or later will seek to expand westward and that eventually will be able to do so.

The argument is a convenient one in many Western countries, where suspicions of Russia have been only calmed, not eradicated, by the collapse of the Soviet Union and the emergence of the Russian Federation, and where waning public support for defense might still be regenerated by appealing to those deeply ingrained suspicions. But the argument is self-defeating. It practically guarantees that NATO enlargement will be seen in Moscow as directed against Russia, thus jeopardizing the chance that Russia will come to recognize a joint interest in stabilizing Europe. And with Russia so visibly a problem to itself rather than a threat to the West, this argument will sooner rather than later run out of credibility with domestic audiences in the West. NATO extension has to flow from NATO's new role, not from Russia's old threat.

Instead of basing itself on old suspicions and assuming that they will be rapidly justified, Western strategy toward Russia must free itself from the mental habits formed in forty years of Cold War. Russia is no threat to the West today and will not be so for a very long time. It is not true that everything is possible in Russia, and that Western policy must therefore prepare for all contingencies. Russia's transition from its present turbulence to any real measure of internal consolidation will most certainly be lengthy. The evolution from the current disarray to the reemergence of a major military force capable of casting its shadow over the rest of the continent will be lengthier still. It is uncertain, however, that the Russia that ultimately emerges will retain the features that have for so long caused fear and suspicion among its neighbors.

Russia's armed forces are destitute and demoralized. Its political system is arbitrary. Its economy is shaky. The rule of law is still in its infancy. The authority of the center vis-à-vis the republics is tenuous. There is much to suggest, including the extraordinary resilience and talents of its people, that Russia will ultimately succeed in the enormous task of modernizing its state, economy, and society. But this will be a matter not of months or years but of decades, and during these decades it will be Russia's instability, not its power, that will cause problems for Europe.

Still, many in the West tend to liken Russia to Germany between World War I and Hitler's rise to power in the 1930s—a nation humiliated by defeat and shaken by economic depression and likely to fall under the spell of some reckless nationalistic dictator who might then proceed to take on the rest of the world. But the defeated and demoralized Germany of the 1920s was already a modern industrialized state; Hitler's dictatorship was possible precisely because he could seize control of all the institutions at the disposal of such a state. These conditions simply do not exist in Russia. Of course, Russia will create problems for the West—by selling nuclear reactors to Iran; by slowing down the dismantling of its nuclear stockpile; by attempting, as in Chechnya, to impose the authority of the center on unruly regions; or by putting pressure on smaller neighbors. But for the foreseeable future, it cannot mount a strategic challenge to the West.

Instead of having to hedge against the threat of a soon-to-be-powerful-again Russia, the West must deal with a weak Russia and address the challenge of continuing Russian instability.

What Place for Russia in Europe?

It might be tempting to deduce from Russia's reduced status that it is no longer necessary for Western policy to accord it special consideration—since the superpower is no more, Russia's influence is at best that of a middle power that neither deserves nor should be offered a special place in the affairs of Europe.

The temptation must be resisted. Russia remains a special problem for Europe not because of its ability to shape events on the continent but because of the damage that its inherent instability can cause. Isolation would exacerbate the problems of Russian instability and the damage that a slighted Russia could do to Western interests, not least in terms of nuclear proliferation. Moreover, since the country is likely to regain major stature, albeit in a distant future, it is common sense to try to draw it into a network of dialogue and cooperation early on. Establishing with the weak Russia habits that will last with a strong Russia—that, after all, has been the lesson of the successful integration of Germany and Japan into the community of the West. Regular and broad-based interaction with Russia's leaders, bureaucrats, and policy elites is also the most promising method for influencing Russian behavior in the interim—and thus for containing the wider risks of Russian instability.

Western governments claim that much of this already is being done and point to the many bilateral meetings and consultations with Russia's leaders and government. Indeed, these efforts are important. Some activities—such as U.S.-Russian nuclear arms control, U.S. assistance in the dismantling of Russian surplus nuclear weapons, or various contacts between Russia and European governments—are clearly best conducted bilaterally. But such bilateral contacts are insufficient and need to be complemented by a multilateral arrangement for two reasons. First, bilateralism is more easily exposed to domestic political pressures within each country. Second, unlike consultations conducted between two partners, a multilateral forum lends itself, through its procedures and institutions, to the kind of day-to-day interaction that would strongly mitigate any sense of Russian isolation and, at the same time, inspire a tradition of cooperation.

At first glance, both Russia and the United States might find this idea unattractive; bilateralism brings back for both echoes of past superpower grandeur, when their summits were watched with awe by the rest of the world and treated as defining events. But both also have experienced how vulnerable such a relationship is to domestic pressures and moods, particularly now, when it is no longer seen as the bedrock of international stability. Brutal acts of suppression as in Chechnya (of which there may well be many more) can now put in jeopardy important bilateral arrangements, just as controversial acts such as Moscow's sale of nuclear reactors to Iran can lead to congressional demands to freeze U.S. assistance programs to Russia. Multilateral institutions are simply more crisis-resilient than bilateral relations. While they cannot and should not replace bilateral efforts, they can provide them with a safety net.

Dealing with a weak Russia, therefore, is best done by including it in a multilateral framework of permanent cooperation and interaction. Such an institution does not yet exist. The OSCE, which includes Russia, will remain a kind of Eurasian United Nations without a security council. The idea, indeed the only one advanced on the issue by Russian leaders so far, of superimposing over the more than fifty OSCE members an OSCE Directorate in which Russia, the United States, and major Western European powers would have the decisive say on matters of European security is intriguing in theory. Yet it is totally unrealistic to expect all the other member states, each of which has a veto, to agree to such an arrangement. Russia is also included, at least partially, in the Group of

Seven (G-7) industrial countries whose leaders meet annually; but this is an event rather than an institution and has proved incapable of evolving into one.

At the same time, Russia remains too unwieldy to fit into any of the major Western institutions, whether NATO or the European Union, although both are committed to taking in new members. The reason for this is not because making Russia a member would deprive the other Eastern European countries of the very reassurance they seek through membership in these institutions, nor because of memories of past Soviet expansionism and repression; these concerns, while serious, might even be best allayed in an enlarged NATO or EU that included Russia. The reason is, essentially, that Russia—due to the magnitude of its problems, its demand for status, and its traditions—cannot be accommodated within these organizations in a way that would permit their continued operation. Russia's membership in NATO or the EU would condemn both to gridlock; it would mean the end of both.

Perhaps one distant day this will no longer be so. A Russia that has overcome all the barriers to the modernization and consolidation of its state, its economy, and its society; a Russia in which the traditions of democracy and the rule of law are firmly rooted; a Russia that has acquired the non-expansionist nature of post-industrial societies—such a Russia would be a serious candidate for NATO membership. But, as the mere listing of these criteria indicates, for the foreseeable future, Russia cannot possibly meet these conditions. For a long time to come, it cannot be integrated into the existing Western structures of European order.

What follows from Russia's inability to fit into these structures, however, is not simply to proceed with extending NATO eastward, perhaps softening the impact, as Western leaders are still tempted to do, by hinting non-committally that Russian membership somehow remains possible. This amounts to nothing less than opting out of responsibility for creating a comprehensive European framework of stability; it invites Russia to regard any Western attempt to provide reassurance to Eastern Europe as an unfriendly act. Indeed, that is the real danger in the way the West is currently treating NATO's extension eastward.

The conclusion to be drawn from Russia's inability to fit into existing institutions must be a different one, and it must be grasped urgently: If existing institutions are not adequate and cannot be adjusted to the need, then a new institution will have to be created to address the task of tying an unstable Russia into the effort to achieve European stability.

Some suggestions of how this might be done have been made in the Western debate—by agreeing on a joint NATO-Russia declaration emphasizing the need for close consultation, by creating a Standing

Consultative Committee between Russia and the Atlantic Alliance, or through a Treaty of Security Cooperation between Russia and the members of NATO. Yet all of these proposals fall seriously short of what is required: for Russia, a place of respect and legitimate influence in a new Europe; for the West and the rest of Europe, a place for permanent dialogue with Russian leaders and elites and for containing the risks of Russian instability.

A NATO–Russia Forum

Rather than through a committee, a declaration, or even a treaty, such a place must be established through a full-blown institution, involving Russia on one side and NATO on the other. Perhaps even better would be the participation of not just Russia but the Commonwealth of Independent States (CIS), the loose cooperative structure established among most former Soviet republics, including Ukraine. This would have the advantages of making Russia feel more equal to NATO and, more important, of giving Ukraine—which otherwise would remain outside the firmer formal structures of European stability—a degree of involvement, influence, and regular contact with the West. Yet since Moscow has long sought Ukrainian subordination to the CIS in security matters, Ukraine may well forgo the advantages of being part of a structured dialogue with the West for fear of being drawn uncomfortably close into Russia's orbit. Thus Russia would probably have to be NATO's sole partner, at least for the time being; and bilateral rather than multilateral arrangements will have to be worked out between Ukraine and various Western countries.

To assure visibility and depth of interaction, the NATO-Russia Forum here proposed would need many of the institutional trimmings that NATO has developed for itself. Possible features might include:

- The Secretary-General of NATO and a Russian counterpart to act as the chief coordinating officers, responsible to a Council of Ministers, consisting of the Russian Foreign and Defense Ministers and their Western counterparts chosen by rotation within NATO, and to a Committee of Permanent Representatives.

- A Military Committee of representatives of the Russian Defense Ministry and the NATO Military Committee to act as the permanent group for exchanging information on military planning and military operations, as well as for preparing joint operations, including peacekeeping.

- A Nuclear Planning Group to address issues of de-nuclearization and nuclear proliferation.

36

- An Arms Control Working Group to look at ways to implement the arms control agenda, including the thorny matter of arms exports.
- A Parliamentary Contact Group to bring together, on a regular basis, a delegation of the North Atlantic Assembly and the Russian Duma.

The point here is not to present a ready blueprint but to demonstrate the plausible scope of what such a formal NATO-Russia organization might look like and to indicate at the same time how it might deal with many Russia-NATO issues currently addressed either inadequately or not at all.

Take the conflict in Chechnya. Today, the West's principal means of influencing that situation are telephone appeals to President Yeltsin, public expressions of concern and condemnation, diplomatic protests, and, if Russia agrees, the dispatch of an OSCE fact-finding and mediation mission. In the NATO-Russia Forum proposed here, in contrast, NATO representatives could have voiced their concerns well before Russian armed forces began their move into the rogue republic. The Military Committee could have analyzed and highlighted the military difficulties, demanded more information, and urged the dispatch of observers, thereby adding weight to the many reservations about the operation expressed by senior Russian military figures. The Parliamentary Contact Group could have called its members together and strengthened the Duma in its opposition to the president's policy. Even if the Russian government had then been unwilling to heed these pressures, there would have been a framework for giving them resonance.

Or take the Russian demand for rescinding certain provisions of the treaty limiting conventional forces in Europe (CFE), which prohibits the movement of heavy weapons between defined geographic zones—in the past a measure of considerable relevance to inhibiting surprise attack. Today it no longer holds that significance, and the Russian demand for a revision has long been plausible. Yet the Western reaction to it until recently has been to play it down and insist on full compliance with the treaty, coupled with some vague promises that Russian concerns would be taken into account in reviewing the CFE in 1996. A Russia-NATO Forum could have helped to defuse the issue earlier by allowing its Military Committee and its Arms Control Working Group to analyze Russia's legitimate military needs, to seek interim arrangements, to examine possible confidence-building compensations, and to work out concrete proposals to deal with the issue. Thus each side could have had the confidence that its concerns were being taken seriously.

These examples illustrate how the proposed NATO-Russia Forum could operate in specific instances. Its greatest value perhaps would lie less in defusing or solving specific contentious issues than in establishing a pattern of permanent interchange on security-related issues. Matters of concern for each partner could be taken up without the inflating and politicizing effect of summit meetings, and in a way that involves not just the top leadership but many governmental layers in the experience of consultation, information, and practical problem-solving.

For the West, working with Russia in such an institution could be the most promising method for coping with the problems and uncertainties of Russia's long journey to recovery. The Forum concept also does raise a number of legitimate concerns.

First, a formal role for Russia in the shaping of European stability would also open Western policy to Russia's influence, particularly in policy toward the rest of Eastern Europe. That concern cannot be dismissed by pointing out that the Russia-NATO Forum would be a consultative arrangement; since it is designed to offer the West formal influence over events and decisions in and around Russia, it will inevitably enhance Russia's influence over events and decisions within NATO, including the ways the Western Alliance conducts its relations with former Soviet allies and republics. There will be many in Eastern Europe, therefore, who will initially accuse the Forum of being nothing less than a Russia-NATO condominium.

This charge cannot be treated lightly. The price of Western influence on Russia's behavior in the NATO-Russia Forum is Russia's influence on NATO governments. Russia could not prevent the West from pursuing its interests; influencing one another does not amount to a veto. Yet the kind of permanent interaction that is a major feature of the new NATO-Russia institution proposed here formalizes and thus intensifies influence. It also opens the chance to try to overcome opposing views. A Russia opposed to, say, Poland's joining NATO would have a better opportunity to put its arguments forward, but so would the West to refute these arguments.

Moreover, exerting influence of course is not dependent on formal institutions; it is more crudely, and possibly more damagingly, practiced in their absence. If Russia wants to block Polish NATO membership, for instance, it can and will seek to influence Western policy by publicly holding hostage issues important to Western governments, such as the ratification of START II. Organizing influence through agreed procedures makes that kind of linkage more difficult because it offers channels for dealing with each issue on its own merits. Similarly, it discourages the public escalation of threats of what one side will do if the other acts in a way it dislikes.

A NATO-Russia Forum therefore would not amount to a condominium of Russia and the West over the states that lie between. Moreover, NATO's eastward strategy would not be limited to the dialogue with

Russia, nor would NATO be limited to its present membership; some of the countries now worried about a NATO-Russia condominium would be represented on the NATO side.

A second concern about a Russia-NATO Forum—farfetched today but nevertheless demanding reflection—is that the new institution could someday replace NATO as the main European security structure. This concern is similar to past Western, particularly U.S., reservations about the OSCE: Would this body not sooner or later make NATO seem expendable? Only when it became obvious that the OSCE was no competition to the Western Alliance were Washington's misgivings laid to rest.

As long as Russia is mired in its internal contradictions and instabilities, the NATO-Russia Forum cannot replace NATO. But what if Russia emerges from its protracted troubles as a vibrant democracy, a post-industrial society not fundamentally different from those of the rest of Europe and North America? In that distant and distinctly uncertain case, it will not make much difference whether the new Russia becomes a member of NATO or the NATO-Russia Forum takes the place of a reformed Alliance capable of also including countries like Ukraine or the Baltic states, for which no adequate security framework today exists. Any institution, NATO included, is transitory. Indeed, the possibility that a NATO-Russia Forum could one day become the basic European security structure may be one of its attractive features—and not only for Russia.

What if Russia Says *Nyet?*

What if Russia's leaders were to turn down the formal arrangement with NATO proposed here? That cannot be discounted. After all, one of the consequences of the West's inept maneuvering over NATO enlargement is that proposals for a more formal relationship with Russia now risk being seen in Moscow as an attempt to buy Russian acquiescence to the inclusion of Eastern European countries in the Western Alliance. How to establish a special relationship between Russia and the West came only as an afterthought once Russia's hostility to NATO extension was realized in Western chancelleries. It will take strong statesmanship in Moscow to accept that a proposal like the NATO-Russia Forum is not a tactical ploy but a genuine attempt to include Russia in a common effort to promote stability in Europe.

Should the West put NATO's enlargement on ice until Russia accepts such a proposal? The answer has to be negative—and not only for the familiar reason that Russia should not be allowed a veto over NATO's plans. Trying to establish a close relationship with Russia must be a major element of NATO's new role. But the failure of a seriously planned and honestly pursued attempt cannot end the West's efforts to secure peaceful change on the continent. If Russia refuses to take up a serious offer to make it part of the new Europe, the new Europe will form without it.

It will form not because of the West's ability to determine the shape of the new Europe but, on the contrary, because of the West's inability to prevent it from taking shape. The westward push of Central and Eastern Europe is a historic one, fueled as much by cultural affinity as by the long and painful experience of Soviet control and the hope of finding prosperity and reassurance with the West. Even if Western governments were determined to maintain the status quo and keep the NATO club closed to newcomers from the East, they could only slow down the westward thrust, not block it. Indeed, that is precisely what Western countries initially tried to do—both NATO's Partnership for Peace and the EU's Association Agreements with Eastern European countries were originally designed to put the issue of full membership on ice. The fact that NATO membership is now on the table for at least some of the new democratic states in Eastern Europe is the result not of the West pulling but of Eastern Europe pushing.

That is why Russia would hurt its own interests most if it turned down a serious Western offer for closer security cooperation such as the NATO-Russia Forum proposed here. Such a move would isolate Russia in Europe and vis-à-vis the West in general at a time when serious strategic problems to the east and south of Russia suggest a particular interest in stability and cooperation along its western borders. Turning down such an offer would also deprive Russia of all but the crudest types of influence at a time when the Western institutions extend their organizational reach toward the countries to Russia's west, a relationship that would be even more closely knit in the face of ongoing Russian hostility. This would scarcely be in the interest of the West or of Eastern Europe; it would be so clearly calamitous for Russia that Russia is unlikely to refuse an offer that prevents it.

Chapter 4

EASTERN EUROPE AND THE NEW NATO

The previous chapter dealt at length with the kind of relationship that NATO will have to develop with Russia because this is the most important aspect of European stability that the West must get right. Yet to date, the eastward extension of NATO to include some if not all of the new and struggling Eastern European democracies has held center stage in the Western debate. From communique to communique, the North Atlantic Council has inched toward what has now gelled into a formal trans-Atlantic consensus: NATO must become involved in providing stability reassurance to Eastern Europe, and this must include admitting countries from this region as full members.

Indeed, extension is essential to the Alliance's continued existence. As was argued in Chapter 2, for the sake of its own cohesion, NATO has to commit itself to the common project of serving as a stabilizing framework for Europe as a whole. It cannot perform this task if it remains an exclusively Western club. Furthermore, NATO would sow the seeds of new tensions if it entered into a close arrangement with Russia while excluding countries that only recently escaped from Soviet control. Thus one aspect of providing stability to Europe consists of encouraging cooperative Russian involvement in the affairs of the continent; the other consists of projecting stability to the countries that lie between NATO's current eastern and Russia's western borders.

Why NATO Must Grow

Expanding the membership of a close-knit alliance that acquired its cohesion during the testing decades of the Cold War is no easy matter. Moreover, projecting stability to the uncertain regions of Eastern Europe cannot and must not be the monopoly of a political-military organization. The role and responsibility of the European Union (discussed in the chapters that follow) will be no less significant, and may even be more so, than that of NATO, since economic and social strains are currently the greatest challenges to stability in the former Soviet zone of control.

The expansion of a military alliance is a particularly sensitive question, as the Eastern reaction to the Western debate of this issue has underlined: Russians regard NATO expansion as a threat—although in reality that threat does not exist. At the same time, some in the West and many in Eastern Europe see NATO expansion as a necessary protection against a dangerous Russia—which also does not exist. There are in addition the awkward questions of how far NATO's commitment can be extended without unraveling the Alliance (which already is experiencing a degree of disintegration) and what efforts would be needed to make such a commitment credible.

And yet NATO cannot shun this task. Because it is the only European institution to which the United States is committed by treaty, it is also the one best equipped to provide reassurance to the continent. And because its ability to project security beyond its borders is increasingly in doubt, it has to be ready to open its borders to others. If the Alliance had shown itself ready and willing to intervene in the Balkan conflict to prevent the worst kind of instability—a protracted war on European territory—the argument that NATO enlargement should only be undertaken if and when Russia threatens any of its neighbors would be more convincing. The Balkan debacle, however, has underscored that safety is best had within, not outside, NATO. It also leaves little doubt that in the case of new tensions that fall short of threatening the whole continent, NATO member states would scarcely be willing to open their alliance to states they had rejected earlier. A NATO policy of promising Eastern European countries support in crises but refusing to accept new members would lack credibility, undermining rather than enhancing stability in that part of the continent.

Limitations of the Partnership for Peace

Recognizing the need to convey NATO involvement to the struggling new democracies of Eastern Europe while simultaneously seeking to delay the issue of opening membership to newcomers, the Alliance announced its Partnership for Peace program at a summit meeting in January 1994. According to that NATO summit, "The Partnership will expand and intensify political and military cooperation throughout Europe, increase stability, diminish threats to peace, and build strengthened relationships by promoting the spirit of practical cooperation and commitment to democratic principles that underpin our Alliance." This was to be done essentially through bilateral agreements between NATO and the partner country, involving consultation, advice, military staff contacts, and joint maneuvers.

It was an intelligent, even elegant, approach allowing for much flexibility in regard to the program's ultimate objective and implementation. Yet limiting NATO's Eastern European outreach to the Partnership's informal contacts, consultations, and joint activities was not a policy sustainable over time; it was bound to raise hope, or fears, that more was in store.

This is not to deny the program's usefulness. By mid-1995, twenty-six countries, including Russia, had signed bilateral partnership agreements with NATO. Numerous joint military exercises are planned and a host of other activities have been organized in which NATO military interact with the armed forces of partner countries.

Meetings are held concerning the transparency of defense budgets, which were always treated by communist countries as state secrets. Seminars are organized on civil-military relations in democratic systems of government and on the need to establish political control over the military. The Partnership for Peace thus encompasses practically all of the activities through which a political-military alliance like NATO can assist the process of democratization and stabilization in the countries of Eastern Europe, short of integrating them into its military command structure and offering them the security commitment that full membership implies.

But however politically expedient, or even (considering the absence of an acute threat) militarily sufficient the Partnership for Peace is, it can be only a temporary instrument for NATO to become engaged on the question of stability in Eastern Europe. The program failed to address not only the matter of whether, when, and how to extend NATO membership to Eastern European countries, but also of how to define NATO's relationship with Russia. Its ambiguity generated uncertainty in Moscow and in Eastern European capitals, inviting Russia to try to block these countries from membership and inciting the latter to regard membership as the only desirable form of future relationship with the Western Alliance. Coupled with the overall devaluation of NATO's "out of area" credibility, the limitations inherent in a program designed to gain time and postpone the hard questions of NATO's eastward extension has had the effect of pushing these questions even more firmly onto the agenda.

Thus less than a year after the Partnership for Peace program was launched with the fanfare of a NATO summit, the issues it was supposed to leave open started closing. While it might have been possible to hedge further, at least for a little while, NATO governments, under the prompting of the United States, decided to commit themselves more firmly. The North Atlantic Ministerial Council, meeting on December 1, 1994, stated: "We expect and would welcome NATO enlargement. . . . Accordingly, we have decided to initiate a process of examination inside the Alliance to determine how NATO will enlarge, the principles to guide this process and the implications of membership. . . . We will present the results of our deliberations to interested Partners prior to our next meeting in Brussels" (that is, December 1995).

In other words, the enlargement of NATO is agreed in principle. Moreover, the Alliance has placed itself under political pressure by announcing that, by the end of 1995, it will not only define the modalities of enlargement but also begin to discuss the follow-up. Claims that NATO is only discussing the "why and how" of enlargement, not the "who and when," may be formally correct; yet the first phase is so clearly the introduction to the second that the latter can be delayed for long only at considerable political cost. Recently, in response to growing manifestations of Russian displeasure, even threats of what Moscow would do if NATO enlarged, Western governments seem to have had second thoughts about the desirability of proceeding along the planned route. They have thus maneuvered themselves into an awkward position: they can no longer refuse or even significantly postpone enlargement without appearing to kowtow to Russia, and they can no longer promote it without antagonizing Russia.

But NATO membership for Eastern European countries is inevitable—nothing less will do much longer. Therefore the questions that need to be answered soon are: Which countries (and which not)? When? And with what consequences for the security commitments, the forces, and the cohesion of existing Alliance members?

Defining NATO Membership

Which countries should be invited to join NATO as full members? The most obvious approach—defining a set of criteria for membership—is also the least sensible. Clearly not all the countries situated in the wide region between Germany, Greece, Turkey, and Russia can and will be asked to join the Western Alliance. That decision, after all, is not a statistical or geographic but a strategic one. Criteria for membership will always be rather general in nature, referring to the solidity of democratic reforms, civilian control over the armed forces, ability to contribute to Alliance defense, etc., all verifiable only by very crude yardsticks. The decisive matter is not which countries meet these criteria, but which countries' membership in NATO will facilitate or complicate NATO's stabilizing objective.

Given the transitory nature of any present security arrangements in Europe, that question cannot be answered once and for all. The answer depends on the circumstances. Estonia, for example, would probably meet all conceivable criteria. But to invite this small country on the border of Russia and with a large Russian minority into the Western Alliance would not only cause massive vituperation between Russia and the West, it would also leave Estonia vulnerable to Russian military pressure that NATO would be unable to do much about. Instead of weaving a network of reassurance across Europe, NATO would increase the risk of major tensions—at least judging by the situation today.

But that situation could change. A Russia assured of its status and engaged in a joint institutional effort with NATO might well look at Estonia's NATO membership differently in a few years' time. In a bit longer time, growing tensions with China might even lead Moscow to appreciate NATO's involvement in Russia's West. In the more distant future still, the NATO-Russia Forum, if it evolved into a finite Europe-wide security organization, would naturally include all of the countries that, from today's perspective, would not be included in NATO even if they met all conceivable criteria.

Thus in the foreseeable future the decision as to which countries to admit into the Alliance must be based not on what may ultimately become possible but on what seems advisable under near-term circumstances.

The likely near-term evolution of Eastern and South-Eastern European countries as well as the likely repercussions of opening NATO membership preclude most of these states from being admitted for the time being. Many are not capable of meeting the conditions of membership soon, while the inclusion of others would risk causing greater instabilities than membership could remove. NATO's enlargement policy therefore has to combine a general, unambiguous commitment to opening up the Alliance to new members with the invitation to a specific few, while at the same time offering lesser forms of involvement to the remainder and making clear that the door will remain open to others when circumstances permit.

The specific few will, not surprisingly, be the countries both closest to NATO territory and farthest down the road to democracy and internal stability: Poland, Hungary, and the Czech Republic (Slovakia also used to belong to this group but has fallen behind because of growing doubts concerning its democratization process). Of these, Poland's membership in NATO will be both the most problematic and the most symbolic. It is, next to Ukraine, the largest country in Eastern Europe. Moreover, given Poland's proximity to Russia's Kaliningrad territory and to a Belarus increasingly leaning toward Russia, Polish membership in NATO will generate much more concern in Moscow than will Czech or Hungarian membership; indeed, Poland has become the focal point of the Russian campaign against NATO expansion.

Yet no other country has Poland's stature as the symbol of the new Eastern Europe. Hence excluding Poland from the first wave of new members would both be incomprehensible to Western publics and signal to all of Eastern Europe that NATO's enlargement policy lacks seriousness and resolve. It would be worse than not enlarging NATO at all.

A Matter of Timing

When should these three countries be admitted? As a general rule, a clear date, far enough in the future so that they as well as all the other players could make the necessary adjustments, would have been best at the outset.

If NATO had early on declared its willingness to invite Poland, Hungary, and the Czech Republic to join on, say, January 1, 2000, this would have provided a perspective with immediate beneficial effects. Applicant countries—aware that membership requires a resilient democracy, a functioning economy, a democratically controlled and modernized military, as well as the peaceful resolution of any outstanding border or minority disputes—would have engaged in that difficult job in the knowledge that these efforts would be rewarded, and their publics would have more readily accepted the sacrifices involved. Their neighbors, above all Russia, would have had time to adjust to the knowledge that NATO's decision could not be reversed. NATO staffs would have been able to work out the detailed military issues that enlargement implies. Alliance governments would have had the opportunity and the time to establish a better relationship with Russia and to convince the public and political elites in their respective countries of the need to take on new security commitments toward yet unfamiliar new members.

NATO's initial indecision, however, followed as it was by a rapid hardening of positions in favor of enlargement and accompanied by manifestations of growing Russian displeasure, has ruled out setting a distant date and working up to it in an orderly process. Ironically, Russia's remonstrations have only furthered the cause of those pushing for rapid enlargement. For if the West would now fix the date of entry as measuredly as it should have done in the first place, this would be interpreted all over Eastern Europe as well as in Moscow as a sign of wavering, of doubts and second thoughts. Hence by its own procrastination, the West has lost rather than gained time.

The consequence is that setting any precise distant date is no longer an option. Instead, the Alliance will have to proceed as it seems now to have begun to do—by defining conditions of membership, identifying the countries whose applications are welcome, and entering into formal treaty negotiations with each of them. The date of entry will then be determined by the length of these negotiations and of the ratification procedures in each of NATO's sixteen member countries as well as in the applicant country.

This is, under the best of circumstances, a much lengthier process than the current Western debate generally suggests. Even if NATO had already assessed all the consequences of enlargement, even if all Alliance governments were equally determined to proceed—and neither of these conditions currently exists—it would be years before a new member could take its place in the councils and staffs of NATO. Even rapid enlargement will be slow.

Implications for the Alliance

All previous enlargements of NATO occurred during the Cold War. Greece and Turkey were admitted in the early 1950s, when the Korean conflict raised fears of an impending war in Europe; West Germany joined in the mid-1950s because its territory and manpower were indispensable for holding off the Soviet Union; Spain's accession in 1982 merely formalized what for long had been a de facto alliance relationship. Due to the Cold War, it was clear in each of these cases that the central commitment of the North Atlantic Treaty, enshrined in its Article V—"an armed attack against one or more shall be considered an attack against all"—would naturally extend to the newcomers. Indeed, their membership was deemed essential to making that commitment more credible for the Alliance as a whole.

Today, the situation is different. The Alliance will be inviting new members not because it wants them on its side to deter any specific present or future danger, but because membership has become an important instrument, among several, for promoting stability in Europe. Yet the Treaty's backbone is the commitment to deter and defend against attack. It would be inconceivable to admit new members and declare that, since no major threat exists, all that the old allies owe the new ones is some kind of stability support. Moreover, NATO is most concretely an organization for joint defense. Membership therefore implies participation in the defense of the Alliance and willingness of the Alliance to defend its members.

The new members must have the same security status as the old. But what this means is ambiguous. The difficulty in applying Article V to the new strategic circumstances of Europe lies not so much in the principle that an attack on one ally is an attack on all, but in translating that principle into practical military commitments. This difficulty applies to both current and future NATO members.

The uncertainty about the extent and nature of NATO's residual military tasks discussed in Chapter 2 pertains also to NATO's military enlargement. What, if anything, is required militarily to signal that a country has become a member? If no attacker is on the horizon, what must be done to show that allies are willing and able to protect the newcomer from attack? During the Cold War, military planners could work with worst-case assumptions, since these contained a certain degree of plausibility. But the worst case—a Russian attack—is no longer plausible. The "security guarantee" is still defined as it was in the past. But how can it be expressed today in practical military terms?

In the debate over this question in the West, many answers are still mired in Cold-War thinking. There is talk of "extending the nuclear guarantee" to new members, of the need to station multinational forces on their territory, of giving "real" rather than rhetorical guarantees. Yet these answers are not compelling. It is conceptually difficult to transpose the "nuclear guarantee" of the past into today's U.S. commitment to even close allies such as Holland, Britain, or Germany; what then does it mean to "extend" it to Poland or Hungary?

As to the deployment of allied forces, the pre-positioning of military supplies, the stationing of nuclear weapons on the territory of new members, even their integration in allied commands—none of this is essential any more. Moreover, there are almost as many different arrangements in the existing NATO as there are current members. Norway relies entirely on reinforcements in a crisis. Neither Denmark nor Norway accepts allied nuclear weapons on their soil in peacetime. France left the integrated military structure in 1967 and is inching back to it only now when that structure is loosening. Only West Germany (not, despite unification, East Germany) has allied ground forces permanently stationed on its soil.

In most cases, these differences result from unilateral national decisions that could also be rescinded unilaterally. But take the case of East Germany: Since it was united with West Germany in 1990 and all of Germany became part of NATO, the treaty of unification that includes the then-Soviet Union among its signatories stipulates that no nuclear weapons shall be stationed and no allied troops deployed on the territory of what used to be the German Democratic Republic.

NATO's considerable tolerance for a variety of arrangements during the Cold War will be even greater now vis-à-vis old and new members alike—provided these arrangements can be altered unilaterally should changing strategic circumstances demand it; this proviso is essential for membership. An excellent recent RAND Corporation study illustrates the rich menu of alternative NATO defense concepts available to the new Eastern European members; the possibilities range from the Alliance's providing only infrastructure, logistic, and communications support, to its providing tactical air power; and finally to its providing full-scale multinational defense deployments (Ronald D. Asmus, Richard L. Kugler, and F. Stephen Larrabee, "NATO Expansion: The Next Steps," *Survival* (Spring 1995), pp.7–33).

Yet however flexible, however minimal or intense, these options beg the fundamental question: What—apart from the degree of reassurance sought by the new members and the degree of assistance the old members are willing to give in peacetime—is the yardstick for defining the military efforts required by both new and old members? What are both new and old members letting themselves in for?

The answer, like so many in these pages, has to be temporary—it depends on the circumstances. For the foreseeable future, the likelihood of an attack is low, and therefore the required allied military investment on the territory of new members is low. All that is needed is an abstract commitment on their part that they will meet all obligations of membership, and some concrete sign that they have acquired a NATO status, such as participating in alliance military staffs, introducing NATO standards into their forces, or taking a regular part in NATO maneuvers. Indeed, this is also what NATO in its 1995 study on the "why and how" of membership has concluded: There is no need for the newcomers to deploy in peacetime NATO forces, not to mention nuclear weapons on their territory in order to qualify for membership. Nor do these countries have to be concerned that the "security guarantee" they receive is less valid than that exchanged between existing members—it is modest for both since nothing in the near future will trigger it.

As Chapter 2 argued, the North Atlantic Treaty commitment today amounts only to the literal meaning of Article V. How allies will react to an attack against one of them will depend on the intensity with which individual members feel threatened and the degree to which they can cope with the attacker by themselves. The kind and level of allied assistance will vary according to the degree to which the threat of attack is shared by the others; possible responses range from the dispatch of forces to the dispatch of a condolence telegram. Each partner will take such action as it "deems necessary to restore and maintain the security of the North Atlantic area" (Article V).

It is this flexible commitment that is being extended with NATO membership—no less but also no more. Article V owes its wording to the reluctance of the U.S. Senate in 1949 to accept anything smacking of an automatic commitment. The flexibility agreed to then is now coming into its own.

This will also enhance the chances of parliamentary approval for NATO enlargement. Because of the new flexibility, the fear is unjustified that the ratification debate in the U.S. Senate over NATO membership for, say, Poland would risk putting into question the U.S. commitment to NATO as a whole. This does not mean that ratification by the U.S. Senate (or any other NATO parliament) is a foregone conclusion; it will require political leadership by the U.S. president as well as other Alliance leaders to have a realistic chance. Yet if the commitment to NATO partners still involved a "nuclear guarantee" to Denmark, Italy, or Germany, the Senate would rightly question not only whether such a guarantee should be extended to Poland but also whether it should be maintained for the allies of old. As it is, Article V makes it possible for the Alliance to adjust to the changed strategic circumstances of lesser threat with a more flexible commitment, just as it facilitates the inclusion of new members in non-threatening times.

The Not-Yet and Never-to-Be Members

Setting up a formal institution for cooperation with Russia and including in NATO's membership some of the new Eastern European democracies will leave most Eastern European countries either in NATO's waiting room or outside. How should the Alliance discharge its stability-building task toward them?

It is here that the Partnership for Peace will have its major and enduring role. Bilateral cooperation between NATO and individual countries can be geared to specific needs and circumstances. The program can prepare prospective members for full membership, and it can reassure the remaining countries of some degree of regular interaction with Europe's chief security organization.

In addition there may be a case for creating a third category of attachment to NATO—associate membership—somewhere between the loose and noncommittal Partnership for Peace and full membership. This would not, or at least not initially, imply any security undertaking on the part of the Alliance. But it would link some countries more formally to its political consultations. It might be particularly suited for those countries, like Slovakia, Romania, and Bulgaria, that could be considered potential candidates for membership but whose time, for a variety of internal and external reasons, has not yet come.

Associate membership for these countries would not only help to underline that NATO's enlargement is not closed after Poland, Hungary, and the Czech Republic have been admitted. The formal participation of associate members in NATO consultations would also make their involvement more familiar to Western audiences and thus pave the way to their eventual acceptance as full members. Finally, it would signal that the Partnership for Peace is in itself a dynamic concept, offering a number of Eastern European countries if not necessarily the prospect of alliance membership, then at least a step to some institutional involvement in NATO affairs.

There would thus be three concentric circles of attachment to the Alliance: full membership, associate membership, and Partnership for Peace, with permeable borders between them, even if not all associate members end up as full members and not all Partnership countries as associate members.

If NATO seriously addresses these various tasks—establishing a formal working relationship with Russia, extending its membership gradually to some Eastern European countries, and weaving a net of cooperation to the remainder of the continent—it will have committed itself to a common purpose that can give cohesion to an alliance that no longer needs to fear a common enemy. It will also lay the groundwork for what could eventually become the new European security system.

Yet the once exclusively Western security alliance can only contribute so much toward assuring that change on the continent proceeds in an orderly fashion and that the chances offered by the end of the Cold War are not wasted. The main problems of the continent are not military but economic and social. Many of these problems will have to be addressed by the other main Western structure of order, the European Union. Whether the EU will be able to take on this task, and how it should go about it, is examined in the chapters that follow.

Chapter 5
A UNION IN TROUBLE

Despite European federalists' assertions to the contrary, Western European integration is a child of the Cold War. Thus it is no surprise that, like NATO, the European Union—the other main Western structure of order—has been deeply shaken by the sudden, unexpected end of the East-West rivalry. This community of Western European states must now prove its cohesion without the glue of a common threat. It must operate in a fluid environment, more on its own than at any time since its inception. And while it previously had to worry only about the economies of highly developed and democratic Western Europe, it now faces the immense additional challenges of having to worry about the prosperity, the stability, and to some extent even the security of the countries toward its east—countries to a large extent still underdeveloped both economically and democratically.

It is true that the concept of a supranational European community in fact predates Yalta. The founding fathers of the extraordinary postwar push to unite the democratic states of Western Europe did not seek justification for their effort in anti-communism or in deterrence of the Soviet Union. The idea was conceived without the Cold War in mind.

Yet the child was born and learned to walk under Cold War conditions. The six founding states could focus first on coal and steel, then on a common market, precisely because the United States and NATO took care of their security; the failure to establish a European Defense Community in the early 1950s was a political, not a security, setback. If these countries mustered the courage to engage in an unprecedented merging of national sovereignties, it was not only because memories of World War II were still fresh but also because of the discipline imposed by East-West antagonism. If the participating countries were able to significantly improve the prosperity of their citizens, it was in large part because the Soviet Union (through its control over Eastern Europe) ensured that the problems of that poorer part of the continent were not a burden for the richer, Western part.

The European Community, founded in the 1950s, thus lived a protected childhood. Claims could be made that did not need to be fully honored. Dreams could be presented as steps toward a new reality. The words that Europeans used were often larger than their deeds, even if their deeds in moving integration forward were without precedent in Europe's history.

The Community's childhood ended with the end of the Cold War and the division of Europe. Even if the Community's leading statesmen sensed the coming change, they did not fully comprehend it. In the last months of 1989, when the walls were crumbling all over Eastern Europe, they decided to bring the Community to maturity by transforming it into the European Union—a change in name relying, once again, on visions to change reality. The Maastricht Treaty, which created the Union, was negotiated in 1991 and became effective in late 1993; it still seems to assume that, although the walls have come down in Europe, other things will remain equal. The Treaty cemented economic and monetary integration among the then twelve member states, thus making the Union a club more demanding for its own members and more difficult for others to join. It left foreign, security, and immigration policies fragmented—the very areas that cause major headaches for the new Europe, a Europe without walls and without the familiar order.

The Incomplete Union

Imperfection of course has been the trademark of European integration; it explains the recurrent frustrations experienced in Europe and the United States over the pace and reach of the integration process. The Union is, after all, a unique experiment, never before undertaken in history—the attempt to pool together sovereign states not only into a free-trade area but into a common market, a common internal market, a common currency, and a common international identity.

In many respects, the EU resembles the confederated United States of America in the years between independence and the Constitution: It is a collection of state entities, each of which has its own army, currency, and tax system, and it has a decision-making procedure in which every state could still veto major changes. But it differs fundamentally from the American experience in that the states it tries to bring together are old countries, proud of their different cultures and traditions, shaped by centuries of separate development and mutual distrust, often achieving their identities through the wars they fought against each other. Even after the devastation of World War II, and helped along by the experience of the common threat of the Cold War, European countries found it difficult enough to jump the hurdles of integration. Now, with these unifying pressures gone, the danger is real that the further hurdles will

seem too high to politicians and that stagnation will lead to re-nationalization.

In this respect, the problems of the EU parallel those of the Western
Alliance. NATO, too, is in drift, and in danger of drifting apart, now
that the unifying threat has gone. But there is a fundamental difference:
in contrast to NATO, the EU has not lost its chief purpose. European
integration is still the best, if not the only, solution to the continent's
problems. For Western Europe, it provides the means of keeping Germany in a common structure that responds both to its own needs and
to the concerns of its neighbors; for Eastern Europe, it offers the opportunity of economic modernization and democratic renaissance; for the
continent as a whole, it provides a framework for prosperity as well as
for making a difference in international affairs. The disturbing issue is
that, while the Union's purpose is clear, the possibilities of achieving that
purpose are now less certain. There is as yet no cause for pessimism—
on the contrary, given the enormous obstacles, the achievements are
impressive and the opportunity the Union represents is immense. There
is, however, cause for real concern.

The Union's purpose has always been political rather than economic. The idea behind European integration is primarily about power,
not prosperity—the domestication of power through the domestication
of intra-state politics and the joining of power to again give Europe a
voice in the world.

This point needs to made, particularly since public manifestations
of the Union suggest that it is guided less by strategic vision than by
technocratic micro-management. However, the objective of European
integration has never been merely a free-trade and free-movement area; a
functioning market has never satisfied what it was really about. European
integration has been defined by a much more ambitious vision—from
the humble beginnings of the European Coal and Steel Community in
the early 1950s (the forerunner of today's Union), to the creation of the
European Community in the late 1950s, to the additional steps toward
integration embodied in Maastricht, to the inclusion of practically all
the developed democracies and market economies of Europe (except
for Iceland, Norway, and Switzerland).

The vision is that war must become impossible between its members; that the rule of law must reign not just within countries but among
them; that Europe is more than just the sum of its national entities; and
that Europe can and must make a major contribution to international
order. The means were economic, but the end was always strategic.
Although there are deep differences today among and within member
states about the end stage of the long way to integration, with some
advocating a looser, others a firmer arrangement, there is less dissent

over the basic objectives than over how to achieve them or over the sacrifices in national sovereignty that they demand.

The Union today is much more than just a common market. The established links between member states today are closer than those between partners of an alliance. It is impossible to imagine that any member country would make war against another; it is difficult, if not impossible, to imagine that an attack on one member state would not be experienced by the others as an attack against them all—not because their own nations would be attacked but because the Union of which they are an integral part would be in danger. In this respect, the Union is a security community—an important consideration, for instance, in Finland's seeking and obtaining admission to the EU (although not yet to NATO).

A Community for the Future?

The European Union prospered in the shadow of the Cold War. With the Cold War's disappearance, however, it faces a decisive test: Can it become the major framework for prosperity and stability in Europe as a whole, complemented by the new NATO? To do so, the EU has to fulfill three conditions that, at first glance, seem difficult to reconcile and may be mutually exclusive: 1) it must enhance the effectiveness of its institutions; 2) it must develop sufficient flexibility to spread the advantages of membership to the less prosperous and less stable countries further East; and 3) it must regenerate public support for European integration.

If the Union does not succeed in overcoming growing institutional gridlock in its decision-making, its authority will decline, public support will dwindle, member states will progressively reclaim powers they previously handed over to EU institutions, and the Community will wither away, opening up prospects for a return to old-time European power rivalries.

If the Union fails to open itself to new members from Eastern and Central Europe, it will lose the chance to encourage stability there and will make itself vulnerable to the divisive impact of social, ethnic, and even military conflicts in that region. This would inevitably raise the German question in Europe again: If the Union were to remain a Western European rich man's club, Germany would have little choice but to proceed on its own in addressing the problems on its eastern border— the worst possible way to deal with those problems and the surest way to estrange Germany from the rest of Western Europe. Moreover, the fallout from Eastern European turbulence—whether mass emigration, widespread crime, or the creeping effect of peripheral conflicts—will not affect Germany alone. It will undermine the rest of the Union as well, generating new divisions and restrictions within it. It would be the ultimate irony if the problems that the barriers of Soviet repression in Eastern Europe once kept away from the Western part of the continent now led to the rebuilding of barriers between the members of a Union designed to remove them.

Finally, if the Union fails to regain support from the citizens of its member countries, all further progress will be blocked and all its achievements will be at risk. There is a sense of doubt throughout Europe today; integration—which for decades was welcomed as a way to compensate for the defects of the nation state —is now often perceived as creating dangers against which the nation state must offer protection. The lifting of border restrictions was fine until criminals and immigrants started to profit from free movement as well. Common policies were acceptable when they gave but did not take away. The European Parliament was tolerable as long as it did not encroach upon the prerogatives of national parliaments. Now, however, Union decisions are beginning to affect citizens directly; the Brussels bureaucracy often appears intrusive; and the EU's opaque decision-making procedure—there are now some twenty different legislative mechanisms—is increasingly disenchanting. Public opinion, which for so long supported serious efforts to advance European integration, has become wary in many member countries.

The Institutional Imperative

Yet in its present state, the Union is incapable of meeting any of these challenges—assuring efficient decision-making, extending membership to Eastern Europe, and regaining the support of Europe's citizens. It is divided about its very purpose between those who favor a closer union and those who would like to see national control maintained and regained. The division not only separates some member governments from others, most notably the British Tory government from those in most EU countries; it also runs within each member state. Hence the thrust toward supranational institutions is weakening, and the return to intergovernmental horse-trading is accelerating. The institutional gridlock that is closing in on the Union and will become tighter with every new member admitted can only be overcome if that trend is reversed and the ability of each member to block decisions by a veto is seriously curtailed.

This prospect is dangerous because it concerns the essence of European integration. Traditional intergovernmental bargaining is based on the premise that unless all agree, nothing will be done. EU decision-making procedures were designed to avoid that. It is true that these rules still leave the decisive word to governments. But they give the first word, the right to initiate legislation, to an organ insufficiently described as the Union's executive body, the European Commission, which must propose the decisions they require; they in many instances require the approval of the European Parliament; and they leave the last word to an independent Court of Justice. Thus an element that is not entirely responsible to or dependent on member governments has been woven into the process by which the Union acts. In this supranational element lies the secret of its past success.

Every enlargement of membership threatens the supranational element, as does the trend toward re-nationalization. If every member retains a veto and more countries join, more can block a decision. From its six founding members, the Community/Union has progressed to fifteen today, and it has already agreed in principle to the accession of a further eight, possibly twelve, in the next two waves. As it spreads out geographically to South-Eastern, Central, and Eastern Europe, it also has to encompass a growing variety of national interests, making agreement even more difficult than the mere number of states involved implies. Already, given increasing differences between member states on many issues, the Union's Council of Ministers is being bogged down in micro-management; it is difficult to imagine how it could function at all once the Union is significantly enlarged.

Hence the European Union is in crisis and the experiment of integration is in danger—as is, therefore, the Union's ability to serve as a central structure of European order. A Union that has not overhauled its institutions will admit new members at its peril; yet a Union that does not bring in the new democracies of Eastern Europe fails in its historic and strategic task. A Union that does not strengthen its institutions before enlargement is unlikely to be able to do so afterward; yet a weak Union will provide neither stability to Eastern Europe nor cohesion to Western Europe, inviting instead old fissures of national rivalry to erupt again. A Union with more effective decision-making procedures, including more majority voting in the Council of Ministers, will pose even greater problems of democratic accountability; yet a Union stymied by institutional gridlock will lose what public support it has so far enjoyed.

How can this circle of contradictions be squared? Theoretically, the answer is easy: the Union should move quickly from its present vulnerable state to a full-fledged federation, just as the American Articles of Confederation were replaced by the U.S. Constitution. The Council of Ministers should be turned into some kind of Senate in which member states are represented, the European Parliament should acquire the powers of any national parliament, and the Commission should become the executive organ controlled by both. Then cohesion would be assured, enlargement would not portend dilution, and public support would be won back.

It goes without saying that this is sheer utopia. The economic and political integration of the states of Europe will not happen in a big leap but only in steps. Invariably, these steps will be shorter, and longer in coming, than required. Yet the efficient functioning of its institutions is the central issue for the Union's future today, much more so than widening its competencies or improving its highly imperfect system of democratic controls.

A widening of competencies is necessary for efficient functioning where the Union already holds responsibilities that can only be discharged properly with additional powers—for example, a joint immigration policy and better coordination of police forces must complement freedom of movement inside the Union. But at this stage of its development, and given disagreement within the Union of what final form it should take, attempts to transfer additional policy areas from the states to the Union will only be counterproductive.

Many proponents of European integration believe that the foreign policies of member states should be brought under firmer, better coordination; they point to the public's disenchantment with the European idea following the Union's failure in the Balkan conflict and to public opinion polls suggesting strong support for a common defense and security policy. Yet there is no common European foreign policy, and there will not be one worthy of that name for a very long time.

The Maastricht Treaty, it is true, has laid down a complicated procedure through which member states can decide that some foreign policy issues should be addressed in common. However, in two years, that procedure has produced only seven modest initiatives, among them the dispatch of election observers to Russia and to South Africa and the establishment of an EU Administration in the Bosnian city of Mostar. Its most ambitious program, the so-called Stability Pact (under which Eastern European countries are asked to make bilateral commitments to their neighbors that they will respect borders and honor the rights of ethnic minorities) has had some effect but would scarcely have been essential: Eastern European governments have been told repeatedly by both NATO and the EU that they need not apply for membership unless these issues have been sorted out. The common foreign policy in this instance consisted of providing a formula for what governments had committed themselves to doing anyway.

This meager performance is not, however, surprising. Foreign policy is still regarded by many of Europe's old states, often with an imperial past and memory, as one of the last reservoirs of national sovereignty. Moreover, as the European disarray over Yugoslavia proved once again, foreign ministry bureaucrats are habitually trained in the art of elevating minor differences into major ones of incompatible national interests.

Objectively, the foreign policy interests of the Union's members do not much differ. Significantly, in the important area of international trade, member countries have long entrusted the task of negotiation to the European Commission. In the more traditional and often less central areas of foreign policy, however, many European national foreign ministries jealously protect their prerogatives, regarding mutual consultation as the highest degree of policy coordination. It makes little sense to invest much energy in breaking this tradition. Even if some dents in it could be made, this would not create a Union acting credibly on the international stage; instead of favorably impressing the public, this approach would only deepen its misgivings.

Can public support for European integration be won back by introducing more transparency and better democratic accountability into the Union's decision-making procedures? Governments, worried by a growth of Euro-skepticism in their countries, have tried this tack recently in two ways: by strengthening the European Parliament and by highlighting the principle of subsidiarity, which stipulates that the Union should be responsible only for issues that cannot be addressed more effectively at the national, regional, or even local level. However, the European Parliament is insufficiently suited to address the basic problem of democratic accountability, and the subsidiarity principle is often more a subjective than an objective criterion.

The major problem with the European Parliament is not that it lacks powers (it has acquired quite a few), but that it is too remote from its voters to give them a sense of representation; this problem would continue even if the Parliament were given greater powers. The decision of the late 1970s to elect the Parliament by direct suffrage (instead of, as before, having its members nominated by national parliaments) has turned out to be a costly mistake: it severed the link between members of the European Parliament (MEPs) and national parliaments, still the chief seat of democratic reference in each member country. As a result, MEPs, however hardworking and devoted they may be, float politically in mid-air, and not even greater powers of legislation will bring them down to a level where citizens feel represented by them.

Moreover, any further major increase in the powers of the European Parliament will be seen by national parliaments in all member states, not just Britain's House of Commons, as an erosion of their prerogatives. National parliaments are already beginning to fight back by insisting that ministers consult them before voting in the EU's Council of Ministers, at times even demanding that they be bound by the guidance given them by national parliamentary committees.

Trying to make the Union more democratic by merely increasing the powers of the European Parliament is therefore a recipe for failure. The trouble is that there is no recipe for success either. The democratic deficit will remain a fact of Union life as long as the Union has a deficit in state power. An institution that does not know whether it will one day acquire the qualities of a federation simply cannot offer the seamless web of democratic control enjoyed by mature democratic nations. If full democratic accountability were the condition for continuing public support for the European adventure, it could not be had.

Fortunately, public support is dependent less on the democratic accountability of the Union's institutions than on those institutions' ability to function effectively. In most member countries, the public has generally been supportive of the European idea and remains so. What makes it nervous and even hostile is not integration per se but moves that, in the name of integration, weaken the protection and certainty provided by the nation state without replacing it with something equivalent. This has been the reason for German popular worries about monetary union and for French hesitancy to implement a joint regime of entry visas. In contrast to earlier times when integration was an obvious bonus, public support can no longer be taken for granted. But it can still be won by credible policies.

This is the essence of the institutional imperative. A Union incapable of taking decisions in the domains entrusted to it will lose public support as well as cohesion. The way to overcome its crisis lies not in ambitious plans for new EU competencies, but in making the institutions capable of delivering results.

The Intergovernmental Conference

Although member governments are divided on the kind of institutional reform needed, they have agreed on a procedure to look at the issue. The Intergovernmental Conference (IGC) is to be convened in 1996 and to conclude sometime in 1997. Member governments have also decided not to begin negotiations with any new applicants for EU membership before the IGC has concluded.

Yet the institutional changes required are of such magnitude that a successful outcome to the IGC is doubtful. As if the quarrel among the bigger member states—between those favoring a stronger European executive and those opposing it—were not enough to cast doubt on the exercise, any boost in institutional efficiency would also provoke opposition from the smaller countries. In the past, the smaller states have been among the most stalwart supporters of the Union's system of supranational decision-making, largely because it gave them greater weight than their size warranted. More efficient decision-making would require them to relinquish parts of this hitherto privileged status.

Serious reforms would have to curb drastically every member's right to veto Union decisions except in cases of extreme national interest. They would have to end the practice that every member state, however small, has a national who is not a governmental representative sitting on the Commission. They would have to bring under the constitutional rules of the Union a number of issues that are still under the control of member governments (e.g., immigration policy and police matters). In short, the reforms required would amount to such major constitutional change, both within the Union and within its members, that success would be doubtful even if all member states agreed on its desirability— which they do not.

Any improvements will therefore fall short of what is required. Given this prospect, it would be wise not to set the IGC sights too high. The Maastricht Treaty scraped through referenda in Denmark and France by a whisker; another half-hearted EU treaty would be incapable of mobilizing public support and would face almost certain defeat.

The consequences are deeply disturbing: The Union will not be fit for enlargement. If it admits new members nevertheless, it will degenerate into a traditional free-trade and (perhaps) free-movement area, with inefficiency at the Union level enhancing the trend of national bureaucracies to claw back prerogatives transfered earlier to Union institutions and discrediting the European project at home and abroad. Yet the pressures for enlargement will be immense, practically excluding the option of keeping new applicants at bay until that distant day when all fifteen EU members agree to endow their Union with adequate powers and institutions. In fact, to compensate for the failure of the IGC, governments may even present enlargement as the true sign of EU vitality.

An Avant-Garde to Prevent Backsliding

Instead of papering over intra-Union dissent and thus weakening further what institutional cohesion exists, the first step to overcoming the dissent should be to recognize it. Those who want to move slowly cannot be forced to move faster. But those willing to move more rapidly to common policies and procedures should be able to do so without being hindered by the reluctant ones. If that avant-garde can show that closer integration delivers real advantages, current hold-outs will join at a later stage—just as the six founding members of the European Community once led the way, making Britain and other originally Euroskeptical countries in Europe finally queue up for membership.

The idea of allowing some Union members to speed ahead in order to encourage the rest to follow has been around for some time. Two-speed Europe, à la carte, concentric circles, variable geometry, core group—many of these terms were coined when earlier waves of new members trying to get into the Union caused fears among the old ones that their integration might be endangered. These ideas are again gaining weight today as the Union prepares to open its membership to more, and more diverse, countries. Most important, they have been formally endorsed in the Maastricht Treaty, which provides that a European Monetary Union—with a common currency managed by an independent European central bank—can be formed, probably beginning in 1999, by a core group of countries meeting the necessary criteria, without other members able to block it.

In practice, the monetary union group as well as other conceivable core groups—e.g., defense—would have to be established around France and Germany, which together have provided much of the driving force behind European integration. Indeed, since the founding members of a monetary union will want to ensure its success, they are likely to coordinate other related aspects, such as economic and fiscal policy, much more closely, once they have decided to go ahead. Therefore entry into the agreed Monetary Union—not the Intergovernmental Conference—will be the defining event for the future of the EU.

The basic questions to be answered are: Will France and Germany maintain the exceptionally close relationship they developed during the Cold War years, on which the whole core-group concept depends? And will they be prepared to take the decisive step of monetary union?

The Franco-German Couple

The special ties between these two former European archrivals date back to the Schuman Plan of the early 1950s, the first project of European integration. The initiative was France's, but the emotional context was provided by the young Federal Republic, grateful to be accepted as a partner by its traditional enemy and, as a result, by its smaller neighbors as well. Remarkably, the relationship has held and matured ever since despite major changes: from the France of Robert Schuman to that of Charles de Gaulle, Francois Mitterrand, and Jacques Chirac, and from the 1950s' Germany of limited sovereignty to the Germany of the 1990s, united and fully sovereign. While French elites have found it more difficult than German elites to adjust to these changes, the mutual instinct for preferential relations has remained deeply ingrained in both countries.

Germany's interest in strengthening the special link to France is clear. It rests on the profound conviction of its political elites that the country must never again feel alone in Europe. This, they believe, would lead to isolation. And isolation would invite Germany's neighbors to compensate for German power by weaving countervailing alliances, while in Germany it could give rise to a new, go-it-alone nationalism.

Germans believe that France is the country they can most count on to avoid isolation. The only other country in Europe of sufficient weight to not make a close relationship appear to be covert domination by the stronger partner would have been Britain. Britain's leaders, however, have rarely understood the German need to not feel alone; through their seemingly unlimited capacity to misjudge the political finality of European integration and their related unlimited capacity to turn "Europe" into a running domestic controversy, they have regrettably marginalized their country.

Paradoxically, the reunited and hence even more weighty Germany has now become more, not less, dependent on France. During the Cold War, there was a functioning Western system; now an uncertain, probing process toward new international structures has increased Germany's desire to avoid loneliness. Doubts over the future of NATO and the EU have, if anything, intensified Germany's need for privileged relations with France.

France's concerns are different but, in the final analysis, its interest, too, lies in maintaining and expanding cooperation with its big neighbor to the East. Its postwar strategy of controlling German power by treating Germany as a preferred partner within the European Community while claiming superior status outside it has run its course. France now has three options: 1) to bind Germany through closer integration across the board; 2) to de-emphasize integration and instead form countervailing arrangements with other Western nations, or 3) to combine integration with flexibility.

Although the first option is the most sensible, it is unlikely to win unambiguous favor in France. It was easy for Germans to give up sovereignty to European bodies, since theirs was a limited sovereignty anyway until 1990. For the French, on the other hand, losing freedom of maneuver by casting their lot with others departs from their preferred image of themselves. Moreover, it was one thing to tie down, through integration, the bigger part of a divided Germany; it is very different to try to constrain a united Germany, now the most populous and economically most powerful nation in Western Europe.

The second option holds even less attraction for France than the first. If France is worried about German power, it makes no sense to cut the ties that somewhat control that power in the European Union.

Moreover, there are no weighty potential partners in sight with whom coalitions capable of balancing Germany could be formed.

Thus the third option of combining integration and flexibility is the most obvious choice for France: to proceed, together with Germany, down the road to closer union among Western European states while retaining a margin of maneuver through selective bilateralism—to advance integration and other bilateral interests with Germany; to form a Southern European caucus with Italy and Spain; to cooperate in military technology and peacekeeping with Britain and in crisis management with the United States. This option both keeps the chances for a European Germany and hedges against the risks of a German Europe. It combines Gaullism and Europeanism, the major historic trends in France.

Both Germany and France thus have a strong interest—perhaps an even stronger one than during the Cold War era—in maintaining their "special relationship." Their governments have and will continue to have considerably different views on various aspects of European integration—particularly on the degree of supranationality that is desirable and required; but there is sufficient consensus on protecting the European Union from backsliding and sufficient willingness to proceed together in a smaller group of states to make sure that this does not occur.

The most prominent example will be their participation in the core group of the countries moving to the third phase of European Monetary Union. It is inconceivable that France and Germany will not be among the founding members of this group, determined to ensure the Monetary Union's success by tightly coordinating fiscal, budgetary, economic, and social policies as well. In this sense, monetary union will be the core of political union.

It will not, of course, be easy to move to monetary union. In Germany, there is considerable doubt about—and often outright opposition to—forgoing the strong deutschmark for a European currency. In France, the budgetary austerity required to meet the entry criteria will demand sacrifices that politicians may find too unpopular. Yet these doubts seem soft rather than hard and surmountable by credible political leadership. Moreover, the creation of a European Monetary Union (EMU) is not just a vague goal; it is enshrined in the Maastricht Treaty. For France, failure to proceed would amount to having its monetary policy determined by the German Bundesbank. For Germany, it would amount to what German politicians are trying hard to avoid, namely, the exposure as Europe's major power, and a lonely and resented one at that.

Political leaders striving for monetary union will also not be without powerful allies. EMU, in all the countries that would qualify for participation, is strongly supported by the banking and business communities.

That support has been critical in the past whenever the Union has had to jump a major hurdle. It is likely to help take this one as well.

A Risky Remedy

The "core group" concept is probably the only effective counter to the dilution that enlargement will bring to the Union. The approach does, however, have risks. Introducing a new group or groups within the EU structure, albeit open to the rest, could create new divisions. France and Germany will have to take care that their initiative not be resented as Franco-German dominance. Moreover, only the monetary union group is anchored within the Union's institutional framework; all other core groups will operate outside it, following intergovernmental rather than supranational procedures. Unless core group participants take care to relate their projects to the Union as a whole, their remedy against the stagnation of European integration could well exacerbate it.

If it is true, as this chapter has argued, that the real danger for the future of the EU lies in atrophy through institutional inefficiency, it is imperative to turn back creeping renationalization. Since not all member countries are willing to enhance the Union's structures, there are two alternatives: either for all to accept stagnation or for some to show by example that further integration best serves the interests of Europeans.

Stagnation implies decay, while the willingness of a few to escape from it holds out the prospect of a revitalized Union, capable of meeting the challenges ahead. The most pressing of these challenges—the incorporation of Eastern Europe into the European Union—is discussed in the following chapter.

Chapter 6
EASTERN EUROPE AND THE EU

The enlargement of NATO addresses the concerns of the new democracies in Eastern Europe about external security and responds to their desire to become part of the West. Enlargement of the European Union addresses their concern over internal stability and responds to their desire to be part of Europe.

Inclusion in the European Union has in the past helped countries emerging from authoritarian regimes to make the transition to social and democratic stability; Greece, Spain, and Portugal are the prime examples. But these countries did not present a challenge of the same magnitude as that which the Union is confronting now: to bring into its midst countries whose democratic institutions are raw, whose economies are in the doldrums, and whose citizens, given the painful remedies of the present, remain tempted to seek refuge in the remedies of the past.

Yet the European Union is uniquely suited to meet this challenge. It combines the promise of prosperity with that of political integration; it offers commercial markets and investment as well as a political identity. Moreover, the Union, in contrast to traditional international organizations, does not stop at the national borders of its members but reaches into their domestic structures and procedures, allowing nation-building from within—the only location from which it can be done with any hope of success. It is not a military pact, and thus its eastward enlargement is much less disturbing to Russia; at the same time, the intensity and depth of the links that tie member states together convey a degree of solidarity that borders on common security. Finally, the mere prospect of joining makes it easier for applicant governments to convince their voters of the need to accept the tough adjustments necessary for successful economic and political reform.

Nevertheless, Union member states were initially reluctant to become fully engaged in this new task. Instead of membership, they offered to the more ambitious reform countries in Eastern Europe Association Agreements that would facilitate trade but also deliberately evade the issue of their joining the Union. Only recently have member states recognized the inevitability of eastward enlargement.

At the 1993 European Council of heads of government in Copenhagen, the EU committed itself to inviting countries from Central and Eastern Europe to join and laid down conditions that both applicants and the Union must meet before they take this step. The applicant country's democratic institutions must be stable; the rule of law, human rights, and respect and protection of minorities must be assured; it must have a functioning market economy capable of coping with the competitive pressures within the Union; and it must be able to take on all the obligations and aims of membership, including political integration. At the same time, for the Union, enlargement should not interfere with further progress in European integration.

In contrast to NATO—which has just defined the reason and the modality of admitting new members but will take longer to identify which countries actually qualify and when—the EU has specified through association treaties the countries it considers eligible: Poland, Hungary, the Czech Republic, Slovakia, Bulgaria, Romania, the Baltic States, and Slovenia. It has not yet decided when and how admission will occur. Its strategy consists of two strands: not to begin formal negotiations for admission until the 1996 Intergovernmental Conference (IGC) has sufficiently strengthened the Union's institutions so that they can function with a much increased membership; and, in the meantime, to help applicants get ready for entering the common market through intensive practical assistance.

Partnership for Prosperity

Similar to NATO's Partnership for Peace, the EU has set up what might be called Partnership for Prosperity—a detailed "route plan for the associated countries as they prepare for accession," as the Council of Ministers Report to the European Council of December 1994 in Essen formulated it. A "structured dialogue," covering all Union activities, has been established between the EU and its prospective members. There will be regular, at least annual, but often more frequent, meetings among heads of governments, as well as among ministers of foreign affairs, finance, economics, agriculture, transport, justice, and home affairs. Well before formal entry into the Union, applicants are invited to take part in Union consultations and even decisions on foreign and security policy. They are expected to cooperate "in combating all forms of organized crime" (op. cit.). Current members have pledged increased financial support to facilitate preparation for the newcomers' full membership.

Except for participation in decision-making on the internal and external aspects of the common market and the EU budget, applicant countries are slipping gradually into a quasi-membership status long before negotiations for their formal admittance have even begun. The Association Agreements establish a free-trade area with the Union that is already being implemented, albeit with some restrictions. Already, the EU is the largest import market for Central and Eastern European countries, taking about 50 percent of their exports; EU member countries together are also their largest foreign investor. But the very modesty of those exchanges, as well as the restrictions imposed by the EU on Eastern European exports of agricultural products, textiles, and steel are indicators of the very long road ahead.

Hurdles on the Road

It would seem, therefore, that the Union is well ahead of NATO in opening its membership to the new democracies of Eastern Europe. Unfortunately, this is not the case; the Union trails far behind the Alliance.

This is partly, of course, because membership in a common market, a fledgling political union, and an eventual monetary union involves the pooling of a vast array of activities. For the countries trying to get in, it requires adjustments across the board in government operations and economic performance; for the countries inside, the prospect of having to share the common pie and of facing new competitors raises concern among millions of voters generally reluctant to accept cuts in their material well-being. Membership in a security and military alliance is much simpler to arrange. In addition to these general complications, two specific issues stand out as major hurdles for the rapid admission of Eastern European states into the Union.

The first has been discussed in the previous chapter: the EU's institutions are not fit for enlargement, and it is highly doubtful that the IGC will make them so. The condition that the Copenhagen Summit laid down for the Union—the "capacity to absorb new members while maintaining the momentum of European integration" (Communique of the European Council, Copenhagen, June 1993)—will not be met. The question is whether enlargement will be blocked, or whether it will take place regardless.

Regrettably but inevitably, institutional inefficiency will not stand in the way of enlargement, despite official protestations to the contrary. Committed integrationists as well as pragmatic Brussels bureaucrats rightly argue that an institutionally wobbly Union will be an ineffective one for both old and new members and will fall far short of the cohesive and dynamic political community that the latter hope to join. But, as already noted, these arguments are unlikely to prevail in the real world of politics. The institutional reforms emerging from the Intergovernmental Conference will be insufficient to equip the Union to take in numerous new members—but this will not hold up enlargement. Governments, seeking cover from criticism of the likely failure of the IGC, will, on the contrary, be drawn irresistibly to presenting the admission of Eastern Europe's new democracies as a sign of the Union's vitality. Moreover, in the face of the clear strategic need to bring Eastern Europe into the Union, institutional arguments will soon be regarded as no more than the rear-guard action of petty Euro-ideologues.

For most governments, the decisive barrier to rapid enlargement will not be the Union's institutional inadequacies. Nor will it be the insufficient preparation of East European economies for the common market; while there will be many problem areas, these can be addressed by granting transition periods for specific sectors, as has often been done whenever a new member joined. Instead, the main barrier will be the sheer cost of including new members within the system of subsidies and transfer payments that has been established in the Union and the difficulty of changing that system in time for enlargement.

The outstanding example of this is the Union's Common Agricultural Policy (CAP). To assure a proper income for EU farmers, CAP fixes prices for agricultural produce well above world market levels, puts hefty levies on imports to get them up to intra-EU prices, and subsidizes exports by its own farmers to get their prices down to world market levels. Consequently, the CAP has not only pushed prices up for EU consumers, it has also been a foreign policy nightmare—undermining agricultural efforts in developing countries, where cheap EU imports have driven local producers off the land, and repeatedly souring U.S.-EU relations. The Uruguay Round of trade negotiations under the General Agreement on Tariffs and Trade was the latest case in point: the EU's agricultural subsidy system came close to torpedoing its completion and with it the creation of the World Trade Organization.

Unless changed drastically, CAP will also become a nightmare for EU enlargement. Its costs are already stretching the resources of the Union today, taking up 40.8 billion ECU, or half of the EU's total annual budget outlays. With the inclusion of the Eastern European associates—many of whose economies are heavily dependent on agriculture—these costs would mushroom; if existing rules were to apply to the prospective new members, annual costs for CAP could increase by up to 50 percent.

Although it would be highly desirable, regardless of enlargement, to change these rules rapidly, this will prove nigh impossible given the electoral strength of the farm lobby in many EU countries, particularly France and Germany. Even if governments were willing to go down that road, it would be a long and arduous journey.

The other example of how Union rules obstruct enlargement is the EU's system of distributing financial support from the wealthier to the poorer regions of the Union. These structural funds, primarily to the Southern European member states, now amount to almost 30 billion ECU. If the same rules were to apply when the much poorer states of Eastern Europe join, that amount would have to almost double.

Such amounts will not be forthcoming. The rich countries of the Union will refuse to make significant increases, while the present recipients will oppose the massive reductions implied by sharing the fund with the newcomers from the East. It is not surprising, therefore, that the poorer states of the Union's Southern tier are much less enthusiastic about enlargement than the richer states of the Northern tier. They will agree to the entry of new members only if assured that they will not have to suffer for it. If the CAP is not overhauled radically, if the structural funds are not redefined and redirected, the Union cannot do what it is already committed to: opening its membership to Eastern European states.

Yet even under the best of circumstances, both operations will be drawn-out affairs, constantly hostage to the unpredictability of national elections and the familiar game of linkage in EU internal bargaining— and the best of circumstances cannot be expected. Hence it is unlikely that significant eastward enlargement will take place in this decade. Neil Kinnock, the former British Labor Party leader and since 1995 one of the EU's Commissioners, has estimated that enlargement could take as long as "10 to 15 years" (*Financial Times*, May 2, 1995). It is a realistic assessment. The strategy of assuring stability and prosperity in Eastern Europe through the near-term prospect of EU membership is in real trouble.

Jumping the Hurdles

There are two possibilities for jumping or at least circumventing the hurdles the Union has created for itself against extending membership rapidly to Eastern European countries: 1) granting them partial membership early, with the prospect of extending this to full membership at a later stage, or 2) making them full members from the start but including in the accession treaties extra-long transition periods, during which the overhaul of CAP can be achieved and a new understanding reached on the distribution of structural funds.

The latter approach has been chosen in all previous enlargements and has considerable advantages. The new members would enjoy full membership status once their accession had been ratified, participating as equals in the Union's institutions. It is clearly what the countries of

Eastern Europe wish. Moreover, fixed transition periods would impose on the Union's governments the discipline of a deadline, albeit a distant one, for the reform of its system of farm subsidies and transfers. Self-imposed deadlines have, after all, been one of the traditional and often effective agents of European integration. The only disadvantage of applying this method to the eastward enlargement of the Union is that it will keep applicants waiting for a long time at the Union's door if Western European governments, as they well may, lack the courage to commit themselves from the outset to a precise deadline—even a distant one.

The alternative would be to pursue not full but phased membership. This approach would have many disadvantages. It would create, at least for some time, an ante-chamber membership. If agriculture were excluded from the accession treaty, the newcomers would not enjoy unrestricted access to the internal market: their trade would be checked at the border by EU customs officials, just as it is today. They would at times be full participants in, at other times mere observers of, the Union's decision-making process. Efforts to move to full membership would have to do without the help of a precise deadline and rely instead on the impatience and insistence of the newcomers and the bad conscience of the old members. The only advantage of phased membership is that it opens the door of the Union more quickly—even if it does not open it fully right away.

The answer to the dilemma will have to be a combination of both approaches: partial membership as early as possible, full membership as quickly as possible. The Union must not be let off the hook of having to reform its agricultural support regime; indeed, the prospect of enlargement will provide welcome additional ammunition against a flawed Common Agricultural Policy. On the other hand, the earlier the Eastern European associates find a place within the Union—even an auxiliary place—the better.

After all, even if all the hurdles were removed, the EU's busy agenda for the next few years means that the first associate state will not obtain membership, partial or otherwise, before the end of the decade. The IGC probably will not finish its work before late 1997, and the results are not likely to be ratified by national parliaments and the European Parliament before mid-1998. Enlargement negotiations would start six months later. Even if successfully completed by early 1999, the accession treaties will have to undergo what could be a lengthy ratification process. Not even the best-prepared Eastern European applicant is therefore likely to join the best-prepared European Union before the year 2000, and events along the way could make that date slip further. Since neither is as yet fully prepared, it is likely to take even longer before the first

Eastern European associate sits down as an equal in the EU Council of Ministers.

Thus if the Union waits until conditions are met for full membership, it will fail to respond to the strategic necessity of providing a structure of order for Eastern Europe. This cannot be the right answer.

Instead, the Union must seek to establish quickly as many ties as possible with the associate countries, drawing them more and more into common decision-making, beyond the preparatory activities and the "structured dialogue" that have already begun. While the Eastern European associates could not participate in the integrated internal market, they could participate fully, without a formal treaty, in areas such as foreign and defense policy and crime prevention, in which the Union operates on a purely intergovernmental basis. And whenever matters concerning the integrated market are on the agenda, associate states, while denied a vote, would then at least have the right to be heard in the EU Council of Ministers and the European Parliament.

Such temporary quasi-membership arrangements would have to be accompanied by the rapid lifting of remaining EU restrictions against Eastern European imports. There would also have to be an unambiguous commitment on the part of current members to overhaul the CAP and to provide adequate funding for poorer regions in both Southern or Eastern Europe, with the goal of rapidly removing all barriers to the full and equal membership of Eastern European democracies.

Although this would be less than what many applicant countries hope for, it would nevertheless respond to the strategic motive behind enlargement: to provide, for the new and struggling democracies of Eastern Europe, a framework in which they can find internal and, to some extent, external stability. They would be in the Union's "waiting room" only with respect to economic issues, where differences in the degree of market maturity remain considerable. They would be quasi-members in the foreign policy and security domain, because on these issues the Union has not yet developed coherent institutions and procedures. Through their participation in at least part of the Union's activities, Eastern European countries can hope to add their influence to that of those within the Union who have long sought to reform such barriers to enlargement as the CAP. The EU's Eastern European associates, while not yet fully inside, would at least no longer be outside—and they would have to wait much longer to get in if they insisted on being fully in from the start.

Thus the next decade will be, all at once, demanding, confusing, and decisive for Europe's economic and political integration. Since current member states are not unanimous in wanting to endow the European Union with sufficiently effective institutions, a core group or groups are likely to form within it, initially crystallizing around the European monetary union group but also perhaps extending to immigration and defense. The present Union will itself form some kind of a core group vis-à-vis Eastern European associates that only gradually advance to full-member status. The supranational procedure, once the centerpiece of integration, will be under siege from intergovernmental ad-hocery. Except for the monetary union group, the core groups are likely to follow the intergovernmental route, and the same will apply to sectors such as immigration and foreign policy, where consensus to subject them to the established and successful Community system is unlikely to emerge soon. At the same time, national parliaments as well as national governments will seek to obtain greater influence on the decisions of the EU.

It will be a messy arrangement—dissipating common purpose, undermining cohesion—yet probably unavoidable for negotiating the tortuous road to Europe's integration, which remains the most hopeful prospect for long-term peace and prosperity on the continent. Perhaps at the end of a long period of multi-layered confusion, a new thrust for unifying the different strands within a European constitution will emerge.

The collapse of the Soviet Union has changed the world for both NATO and the European Union. It has unfortunately also undermined their previous concepts and cohesion. Both institutions now have to work out new concepts to assure their future. It is not certain that they will succeed. But if they do, these two central structures of European order will also have to define their relationship to one another, a task both have shunned so far. The next chapter focuses on this relationship.

Chapter 7
THE ALLIANCE AND THE UNION

NATO and the European Union must remain as the two main European structures of order. There are many parallels between them: they have overlapping membership, both have problems of internal cohesion, both are developing responses to the stability challenges further east, both are committed to welcoming some of the new democracies into their midst. And although both have been talking about the need to coordinate their respective enlargement procedures, little progress is visible to date.

Their relationship raises three issues in particular: 1) whether and how the European Union should organize defense cooperation among its members, 2) whether the two organizations should duplicate or complement each other in their enlargement policies, and 3) which organization should enlarge first.

There is no lack of visionary answers to these questions; they are even creeping into the increasingly wordy communiques of Western ministerial councils. European Atlanticists have long held that, sooner or later, the European Union should develop into a European defense community, propping up NATO as the "second pillar"—together with the "first pillar" of North America (the United States and Canada). Many who favor the EU's eastern enlargement maintain that all future members of the Union should also join the Atlantic Alliance.

A paper on European integration issued in September 1994 by the Christian Democrats in Germany's Bundestag—one of the most influential recent contributions to the European debate—stringently links EU extension to the creation of a European defense identity: "The security status in a community of states which regard themselves as forming a union must be identical. That is a condition of membership. If one expects the United States to be prepared not only to uphold its commitment to present Alliance members, but to extend it, at least, to those countries that take up membership in the Union, it follows that Europe has to carry the main burden of its non-nuclear defense. This implies that NATO ultimately becomes an alliance of equals between the United States and Canada and Europe." In other words: the European Union must develop a European Defense Community, and the enlargement perspectives of the Union should define, at least partly, the enlargement perspectives of NATO.

Yet reality is likely to fall short of these worthy objectives. There is no European defense community today, and the road Union governments are pursuing—the West European Union (WEU)—is unlikely to lead there. Moreover, it is difficult to imagine that the United States will allow the Union to define, through its own enlargement, the extension of the U.S. security commitment on the continent of Europe. Instead, the NATO and EU enlargement processes are likely to follow different speeds and include different countries, only partially overlapping, only partially synchronized—and hence even more in need of some coordination.

A European Defense Identity

The EU ties its member states together into a thicker net than any military pact; as noted earlier, it is in this sense already a kind of security alliance. There is no doubt that it is desirable to pool the dwindling military resources and shrinking defense industries of Union governments. The question is how best to do it.

The answer that Union countries have given to this question, even to the extent of enshrining it in the Maastricht Treaty, has been to delegate these matters to a body that preceded the Union and that has, since its founding in 1948, largely led a closet existence: the WEU. Maastricht states unequivocally in its Article J.4: "1. The (Union's) common foreign and security policy shall include all questions related to the security of the European Union, including the eventual framing of a common defense policy, which might in time lead to a common defense. 2. The Union requests the WEU, which is an integral part of the development of the European Union, to elaborate and implement decisions and actions of the Union which have defense implications."

The WEU: Problem rather than Solution

Yet that decision should be urgently reconsidered before the 1996 Intergovernmental Conference solidifies the WEU further. The WEU is not only ill-suited as the vehicle of European defense integration but also counter-productive, both for the EU's enlargement plans and for the European-American relationship on which the fate of European integration continues to depend.

The WEU is not an appropriate vehicle for European defense integration because it has the wrong objective and the wrong membership. Its objective, evidenced in its current priorities, is to undertake military operations if and when the North Atlantic Alliance is unwilling to act. The WEU's planning is all directed at this basically "out of area" task.

Yet, as Chapter 2 argued with respect to NATO, the nature of out-of-area threats is that they no longer (if they ever did) spur all members of the alliance into joint action. The only occasions—probably rare—on which NATO will be militarily involved beyond its borders will consist of "coalitions of the willing," ad hoc groups of member states operating with the acquiescence of all. This will also be true for the WEU.

Indeed, it is nearly impossible to imagine a conflict in which the WEU could muster the unity that NATO cannot. NATO has experienced painfully that, in contrast to the old threat that united, all the new conflicts divide Atlantic unity. This is no different for the WEU. Its members will stand together when their joint security is directly threatened, and they will stand divided whenever it is not. WEU's fault is not that it plans for the wrong conflicts but that it unrealistically assumes it can generate a united response.

The sober truth is that neither NATO nor WEU as such is capable of conducting out-of-area operations; if either tried to do this, it would break them apart. For both organizations, the Balkan conflict has brought this lesson home; like the Atlantic Alliance, which had immense difficulties in devising a common plan of action other than to try to stay out, WEU member governments also were deeply divided over how to define their interests in that war. All they could agree on was for some of them to take part in U.N. sanctions and U.N. peacekeeping—no doubt an honorable activity, but a far cry from a joint out-of-area operation based on the willingness and capability of *all* members to conduct a robust military expedition abroad. Major WEU countries, instead of displaying unanimity over objectives in the Balkans, eyed each others' motives with deep mistrust. If "coalitions of the willing" form within NATO, they will not be defined by WEU membership, nor is it evident how the WEU can contribute to their success.

WEU planning has focused on out-of-area scenarios largely because of the determination of some member states not to encroach upon NATO's prerogatives to organize Atlantic defense. Yet if the WEU is to be "an integral part of the European Union," it must primarily address security and defense of the Union at home, not in some far-flung crisis theater. In other words, any organization to which the Union entrusts its defense must demonstrate its ability to cope with the issues that define the defense of a nation state—protection of the homeland, the organization of adequate forces, joint production and procurement of defense equipment, and coordination of defense and security policies with foreign policy. This does not preclude armed intervention outside the EU's borders. But as in the case of national defense, these exceptional uses of force cannot be the primary motive or the chief criterion for a common European defense policy.

The WEU, however, is neither well prepared nor well composed to address these mundane tasks of defense and security. It is not well prepared because embarking on this agenda would bring it into direct conflict with NATO and its integrated military organization—a conflict that many of its member states want to avoid. It is not well composed because, in recent years, it has opened itself to non-NATO countries, many of them former neutrals, as well as the East European associates of the EU, which, although not yet full members, nevertheless take part in and shape its deliberations.

Attempting to transfer NATO's responsibilities for European defense to the WEU makes no sense. This would dangerously weaken the Atlantic Alliance at a time when it is in the midst of major difficulties. Moreover, the WEU is political light-years away from providing a "second pillar" for NATO. Proclaiming an ambition to do so would read in the United States as a signal that the United States is no longer needed to underpin security and stability on the European continent.

U.S. opposition to the WEU, outspoken only a few years ago, has since subsided; as NATO communiques bear witness, the United States now explicitly welcomes the formation of a European Defense Identity. While it would be hard pressed to define what that identity is, Washington nevertheless seems to have come to the conclusion that the United States should not stand in the way of European plans: if European allies want their "defense identity" to be formally endorsed by NATO, so be it. But given the trend in U.S. public opinion toward introspection and a desire to devolve America's previous world commitments, a European Union claim to be organizing its own defense would now be welcomed by many Americans as confirmation that the United States no longer has to play a major role. The effect would be similar to that at the start of the Balkan War in 1991. Then the European Union eagerly sought to prove its crisis-management capabilities in the unfolding conflict, and a relieved Bush Administration was only too delighted to defer the matter to Europeans. Thus were sown the seeds for the deepest crisis in NATO history and for a festering estrangement between the United States and some of its major European allies. Have those pushing for a larger role for the WEU forgotten that lesson?

A Europeanized NATO

Moreover, there is less need today than previously for a European caucus within NATO because NATO is being Europeanized anyway. When the United States was the obvious and willing leader of the

Alliance, the idea that European governments should coordinate their views outside the NATO machinery had certain merits and was essentially harmless. It encouraged governments long used to leaving strategic considerations to the United States to think through some of these issues themselves. And it helped to counter recurrent U.S. suspicions that Europeans were not carrying enough of the common burden. Indeed, the major contribution of the European Caucus was compiling a list of the burdens Europeans were shouldering to be used with effect by U.S. presidents to counter critics in Congress.

Now such a European body would be not only harmful, for the reasons given above, but also unnecessary. European governments no longer have to balance U.S. dominance in the Alliance; on the contrary, they have to keep the United States involved. NATO is effectively being Europeanized. NATO's agenda will be dominated by European issues rather than global strategy. While the United States will sometimes take the initiative, its engagement will in general be highly selective. In most cases, NATO initiatives will have to come from European governments if they are to be taken at all. As the United States is decreasing its role, the role of European members is inevitably increasing. With NATO's eastward extension, this trend will be emphasized further.

Once again, the Balkan conflict has demonstrated these changes vividly. Because the United States refused to dispatch ground forces to the area, the bulk of the U.N. peacekeepers was provided by West European NATO allies. Washington, for most of the duration of the conflict, took a back seat in NATO decisions, basically deferring to France and Britain, the major force contributors. The conflict that has dominated the NATO agenda since 1991 has not only affected the substance and procedure of NATO decision-making but also its venue.

In June 1995, following a misguided NATO attack on Bosnian-Serb ammunition dumps, the Bosnian Serbs took U.N. "blue helmets" hostage. When Alliance ministers responded by endorsing a Franco-British-Dutch Rapid Reaction Force for the protection of U.N. peace-keepers, they did so in Paris rather than in Brussels at NATO's headquarters—a symbol of the Europeanization of NATO if ever there was one. The fact that the United States later took the initiative for a negotiated settlement—after the Croatian victory in the Krajina in August 1995 had changed the strategic equation—only confirms that the America can still take the lead; it does not prove that it will do so regularly.

The Balkan conflict, it is true, is taking place in Europe. Extra-European conflicts in which the United States became actively engaged would run against the trend of NATO's Europeanization—as was the case in the Gulf War. But these kinds of conflicts are unlikely to reverse that trend, if only because of their rarity. First and foremost on the normal agenda of NATO Ministers, Permanent Representatives of the Alliance's Military Committee, and Commanders-in-Chief will be events in Europe. They always have been, of course. But in the Cold War days, the focus on Europe was the centerpiece of a global strategy; now the focus on Europe is the essence of a regional strategy. The Europeanization of NATO is its natural consequence. That also implies that there is not much need for the WEU as the coordinating body for European NATO members; they can coordinate more effectively, and with less political cost, within NATO.

The WEU is also ill-equipped to meet needs that NATO cannot, such as the practical pooling of European defense resources. This inability is being institutionalized by its peculiar composition, which rolls together four different types of affiliation: *full members*, that is, countries that are members of both NATO and the EU; *observers*, countries that are members of the EU but not of NATO (e.g., Ireland); *associate members*, European countries that are members of NATO but not of the EU (e.g., Turkey, Iceland, and Norway); and *associate partners*, countries in Eastern Europe (including the three Baltic states) with which the EU has entered into Association Agreements.

This complicated composition makes sense only (if at all) as a signal of political aspirations—not as a framework for practical defense cooperation. Not even the WEU's full members see eye to eye on the desirability of pooling their defense efforts, and the WEU's wider array of observers, associated members, and associate partners would add little except confusion to such attempts. The WEU has taken in members and affiliates to demonstrate that it continues to exist and that it matters. This has reduced the likelihood that it can matter where it really counts.

That is no happy conclusion. The WEU is not suited for organizing European defense, but that task needs to be done. Ideally it should be addressed within the framework of the European Union itself, with defense as legitimate an area for European integration as trade or agricultural policy. European defense policy should be subject to the EU's decision-making system and include participation by the European Commission, with specific requirements for majority voting in a Council of Defense Ministers; and reserve for each member state the right of veto with respect to the use of its military forces.

But few European Union members are even considering granting such authority to the EU's institutions. Defense, after all, remains for some of the major EU countries one of those last areas of sovereignty with which they are reluctant to part. Moreover, some former neutrals that have just taken up membership in the EU—Sweden, Finland, and Austria—are unwilling to give up the semblance of neutrality even if it is now denuded of any strategic content and contradicts the compact of solidarity they have entered by joining the EU.

A Core Group for Defense

For countries willing to develop a common defense, there is no other way to do so than in a core group within the European Union that is open to others who wish to join but not blocked by those who do not. The organizing framework for such a core group is already in place; the Eurocorps, the largest multilateral Western military unit, will be operational in late 1995 and includes most, if not all, of the countries that might be willing to develop closer defense ties within the Union: France, Germany, Spain, Belgium, and Luxemburg.

The practical aspects of pooling defense resources will have to be handled jointly if the Eurocorps is to become a truly operational unit. Its equipment will have to become compatible, implying a joint agency for defense production and procurement (which is already under consideration). Training and operations principles will have to be defined, demanding intense interchange between the chiefs of staff of participating nations. Means for communications, joint reconnaissance, and intelligence will have to be developed. (France and Germany are already planning a joint reconnaissance satellite.) There will also have to be some form of political oversight by the defense ministers of Eurocorps countries that does not yet exist. One of the Eurocorps' major handicaps is precisely that its founders did not provide it with a political authority representing the core group of EU countries willing to become engaged in common defense; instead, the Eurocorps has been made subordinate to the WEU, a body inherently incapable of authorizing its use.

Organizing European defense around the Eurocorps would have many advantages—and none of the disadvantages of the WEU. For one thing, it could count on a higher degree of consensus among participating countries than the WEU, linked as these countries are in day-to-day military cooperation. For another, given its limited task, the Eurocorps would not appear to be a competitor to NATO, thus neither complicating relations within the Alliance nor creating an impression in American eyes that the United States was no longer needed or wanted in Europe.

Using the Eurocorps as a nucleus of European defense integration would not be without problems. Yet letting practical efforts define organizational structures rather than seeking tasks for existing organizations corresponds to the original recipe of European integration, the Monnet method that led to the Common Market via an institution designed to cope with coal and steel. In European defense, too, it makes good sense to start with the nuts and bolts. Those seriously concerned with making it work should try to sever the link between the WEU and the EU that European governments so thoughtlessly established.

Eastward Extension: Separate but Parallel

The other aspect of NATO-EU relations that must be addressed is how to coordinate the steps that each of these two organizations is taking to invite Eastern European democracies into their midst.

Ideally, EU enlargement should precede NATO extension. There is no major threat on the horizon that would require shoring up the defenses of potential applicants in Eastern Europe. Since instability has its roots in social and economic tensions in Eastern Europe, the EU's Partnership for Prosperity is, on the face of it, a more appropriate answer than NATO's Partnership for Peace. The process of obtaining EU membership is also politically less divisive for the neighbors of successful candidates than NATO membership: in the former case, neighbors can hope that they may be next; in the latter, they may fear that they are excluded.

Moreover, there can be various stages of EU affiliation—from association to partial to full membership. Membership in a security alliance is a more rigid affair. Finally, EU membership of, say, Poland would bring that country "into the family," thus preparing public opinion in the United States and Europe for the extension later on of the West's security commitment and facilitating the eventual ratification of the accession treaty.

Yet such ideal conditions simply do not exist. As outlined in Chapter 6, the enlargement of the Union will take longer than that of NATO. If a country had to join the EU before it qualified for NATO, there would be no NATO enlargement in the foreseeable future. But the juxtaposition of prosperity and security is misleading; a sense of security is often the precondition for tackling painful economic reforms as well as for attracting the foreign investors who are indispensable for the economic future of Eastern Europe. NATO and the EU cannot pass the buck to each other; just as NATO's enlargement cannot be an alibi for the EU's dragging its feet, so the EU's hurdles to enlargement cannot justify NATO inaction.

Instead, the two enlargement processes should reinforce and complement each other. NATO and the European Union should employ the means available to them to enhance, not complicate, the common goal of promoting European stability.

This will require greater discipline from the EU than from NATO, and more discipline than the EU has so far displayed. Because NATO enlargement implies the extension of existing security commitments, the Western Alliance will invariably display caution when it comes to the number of countries it seriously wants to consider for membership. The European Union, on the other hand, has not been cautious in its selection: not only Poland, Hungary and the Czech Republic, but also Slovakia, Romania, Bulgaria, Slovenia, and the three Baltic states are envisaged as full EU partners sometime in the future.

It is true that no date has been set, and entry into the European Union will in many cases be delayed well into the next century. But the EU has served notice whom it intends to invite, not just into the common market but also into a security community, as these countries' association with the WEU signals. Legally at least, the WEU is even more strongly committed to the protection of its members than is NATO. In case of an attack on one member, the WEU Treaty stipulates assistance by the others "with all the means at their disposal, military and other-wise" (Article V of the Treaty Establishing the West European Union, as modified in 1954), in contrast to the North Atlantic Treaty, which requires allies to do only as much as they deem necessary under the circumstances.

This is another indication of how little strategic thought has gone into the elevation of the WEU as the "integral part" of the European Union. It would be much better to capitalize on the non-military charac-ter of the Union, complementing NATO's enlargement by extending the solidarity of the Union to countries like the Baltic states whose inclusion in the Western Alliance is either not credible or, because of predictable Russian reactions, potentially damaging to European stabil-ity. While Russia so far seems to view EU eastward extension as beneficial and benign, this could turn into suspicion and hostility the more the EU waves the WEU flag.

It also is bound to raise U.S. concerns about EU enlargement. If the WEU commitment to "using all means at their disposal" is serious, then U.S. allies within the EU are granting a security guarantee that could trigger the U.S. NATO commitment, particularly since the EU for a long time will lack the military capacity to honor such treaty obligations alone. These U.S. concerns have already been expressed unequivocally: when Sweden, Finland, and Austria joined the EU in 1995, the United States warned them not to apply for WEU membership at the same time. If they had, WEU members would not have been able to refuse—but the United States would have found its security obligation extended without its consent. If NATO at the time was able to avoid what could have turned into a major controversy, this was due to the caution of the European neutrals, not to that of America's traditional allies.

Different Tools for Different Problems

The lesson is clear: NATO enlargement is the more rigid and EU enlargement the more flexible instrument for promoting stability in Eastern Europe. Instead of out-doing NATO as a military security arrangement, the EU must concentrate on what it does best: providing non-military security, facilitating economic reform, enhancing the rule of law, encouraging respect for minorities, defusing ethnic disputes, opening its markets to the products of reform countries, and promoting foreign investment. Through the device of partial or phased membership discussed in the previous chapter, moreover, the EU, in contrast to NATO, has a wide array of possibilities for bringing Eastern European democracies into its deliberations before they become formal members. The EU must capitalize on these strengths in its strategy of enlargement.

Coordinating the two enlargement policies of NATO and the EU is, therefore, not just a question of mechanics or of who goes first. In all likelihood, Poland, Hungary, and the Czech Republic will be fully in NATO before they are fully in the EU—not because it is better for NATO to go ahead, but simply because it is easier to accomplish and cannot now be delayed much longer (for the reasons advanced in Chapter 4).

Nor can there be total overlap between the future memberships of the two organizations. While it is difficult to envisage that a European country joining the Atlantic Alliance will not also become a member of the EU, this is not true in reverse. Indeed, some of the EU's prospective Eastern European members—the Baltic states, Romania, Bulgaria, or Slovenia—are unlikely to become NATO allies.

Contrary to what is often postulated in Europe, future EU members will not enjoy the same Alliance status. This will apply only to the core group of states that are, or are likely to be, also in NATO. Perhaps that group will expand over time. For the foreseeable future, however, some Eastern European countries will be outside NATO and inside the EU. A successful enlargement strategy by both demands that this difference not be papered over but made explicit.

The preceding chapters have argued that NATO and the European Union remain the primary structures of order and peaceful change in post-Cold War Europe, and that both have to further stability beyond the circle of their current members. The fundamental condition for succeeding in this task has been mentioned in passing but needs to be addressed squarely now: the revitalization of the Atlantic community on which both NATO and the EU continue to depend. This is the subject of the next chapter.

Chapter 8
THE ATLANTIC CONNECTION

S ecurity continues to be—as it has been for over half a century—
the primary interest of both Europeans and Americans in maintaining
the trans-Atlantic link.

If the link were severed, the security of both the United States and
Europe would be impaired. If the United States turned its back on Europe,
NATO would collapse and the European Union would be strained to
the point of disintegration. Germany would stand out as the dominant
power in the West of the continent, and Russia as the disturbing power
in the East. The United States would lose much of its international
authority as well as the means to help prevent European instability from
igniting international conflict once again.

If the link is maintained, security on both sides of the Atlantic
will profit—whether in terms of confronting the dangers of nuclear
proliferation, organized crime, ecological devastation, or the old threat
of regional crises in and around Europe. In an uncertain world, it is
better for both not to be alone.

The problem, however, is how to make sure that this common
need will be met. Since 1949, when the Atlantic Alliance was founded,
NATO has been its natural and adequate expression. Today, it is no
longer sufficient. The specific threat that NATO was created to deter
has disappeared, and if it ever should reappear, it will be in a future
too distant for assuring Western cohesion in the meantime. The new
dangers, as argued in Chapter 2, are indirect and ambiguous, more often
producing division than unity among NATO members.

Even if NATO is adapted and revitalized through the new task of
supporting stability and orderly change not just in Western Europe but on
the wider continent—thus instilling in its members a new and demanding
common purpose—it has become too narrow a beam to carry the trans-
Atlantic roof. Instead, NATO will have to be complemented by additional
U.S.-European institutions, both to ensure its own survival and to ensure
a resilient trans-Atlantic relationship for the future.

Interests without Structure

If interests were enough, structure would be expendable. Europeans know that the continuous involvement of the United States remains the essential condition for their security. Americans have twice in this century experienced that European instability undermines their stability.

Europeans and Americans know that they are, in international terms, each other's significant other. This also explains why they are so frequently frustrated with each other. They hold each other to standards of domestic and international behavior more stringent than those either applies to any other society. American Euro-fatigue is often the result of misgivings that Europeans do not behave like Americans think they should; European anti-Americanism often springs from European resentment that Americans are not like Europeans. Both treat each other with an expectation and an affinity that neither has toward other countries or regions.

No other two major regions are as closely intertwined politically, economically, and culturally. For fifty years, the North Atlantic Treaty has committed the United States to the security of Western Europe; its organization and integration have created a common culture of thinking about military and security matters. Political consultations across the Atlantic have become second nature to bureaucrats on both sides. Trade relations are both blossoming and remarkably balanced, and each region undertakes most of its direct investment in the other. With the spread of English, language barriers have largely disappeared; with the dominance of U.S. electronic communication products, cultural barriers are being wiped aside.

Moreover, Europeans and Americans generally see eye-to-eye on more international issues than either of them do with any other region of the world. They agree on the need to expand respect for human rights; to assure the non-proliferation of means of mass destruction; to protect their societies against drugs and organized crime; and to further the advance of democracy. Both want to strengthen the new democracies in Eastern Europe, encourage reform in Russia, fight international terrorism, and promote peace in the Middle East. While there are differences—particularly over the best way to reach many of these goals—consent, not dissent, is the underlying feature of trans-Atlantic relations.

Why then is the absence of major trans-Atlantic institutions, other than NATO, a problem requiring a remedy? The answer is simple: only institutions can assure the victory of interests over irritations. This is particularly so in a period in which security interests abroad are easy to state in general but difficult to translate into common action, in which economic competition will lead to major friction, and in which trans-

Atlantic irritations will be on the rise, no longer held in check either by consciousness of a common threat or by the pro-trans-Atlantic bias of the generation formed by World War II and its aftermath.

Economic competition will be a major contributor to this process of estrangement. True, Europe and the United States are each other's major trading and investment partners today. But it is an illusion to count on trade and economic interchange to produce, by themselves, a sense of comity. On the contrary, trade means competition, and competition means the survival of the fittest; for the not-so-fit, it usually means a shrinking market share and a loss of jobs. Moreover, trade connections can be woven and broken, money will follow profit, and profit will prevail over affinity. A structure expressing interests that are superior to those of an individual company or investor is needed to manage the strain that economic competition generates and to establish the confidence required for long-term investments. European-American trade and investment flourished in part because these conditions were in place over the past fifty years.

Today, the sense of belonging is still evident. But it is reminiscent of the sand cakes children bake on the beach: once the bucket into which the sand was pressed is removed, they hold together for only a short while. The fear of Soviet power pressed Western Europe and North America into a cohesive form for half a century; now it has been removed like the bucket from the sand. The appearance of cohesion will be short-lived.

Publics and elites on both sides of the Atlantic are becoming less inclined to bother much about understanding each other. This trend is less marked in Europe than in the United States—probably because Europeans, thanks to the longstanding institutional links among them, have come to accept interdependence with their neighbors as a normal phenomenon; their parochialism, at least, extends to the borders of the European Union. Because Europeans are more vulnerable to external turbulence than the United States and conscious of this, the need to maintain close relations with the United States is more tangible for them than the need to maintain close relations with Europe is for Americans. Yet the difference between the indifference felt by European and American publics toward events beyond their respective borders is one of degrees, not orders of magnitude. Left to itself, the sense of shared destiny that still, in a lingering sort of way, holds Europe and the United States together is bound to disappear.

Just a Lack of Leadership?

Those who argue that U.S. leadership can somehow resurrect this sense of shared destiny miss three central points. First, for leadership to provide a framework of action that allies can follow requires maps and compass, clarity of purpose, and certainty of objective. No doubt, successive U.S. administrations have often failed to provide the predictability and determination necessary for effective leadership. But it is not the fault of the Bush or Clinton administrations that many of the old bearings of international affairs have been lost. Nor is it in the power of a U.S. president to recreate them through "leadership." In response to specific challenges—such as the Iraqi attack on Kuwait, nuclear proliferation in East Asia, or a belated peace effort in the Balkans—the United States still can, and often may, lead the way. But no act of American will can reestablish the clarity of the Cold War.

Second, leadership is a self-denying exercise, demanding least of all the ability and willingness to issue orders but instead that to build support, arrange and strike bargains, nudge allies along. Even if Europe were willing to follow, the United States understandably would be unwilling to shoulder, in normal circumstances, those burdens of leadership that it has borne so impressively in abnormal ones.

Third, leadership is not an alternative to institutions; instead it requires them. Take two success stories of U.S. leadership—the protection of the West in the Cold War and the 1990-91 Gulf War. Without NATO, U.S. leadership during the Cold War would have been wobbly improvisation. There would have been no procedure for sounding out allies and making U.S. views acceptable; there would have been no machinery for preparing common positions and for keeping track of national commitments; there would have been no military integration. Similarly, in November 1990, without authorization from the U.N. Security Council to use force to evict Iraqi troops from Kuwait, the Bush Administration would have faced immense political risks in the Gulf War: the Senate vote on U.S. military action could have gone against the Administration, instead of just scraping through as it did, and it would have been much more difficult to organize and hold together the troop-providing international coalition as well as to justify military intervention at home and abroad. Leadership, as military commanders have always known and these examples confirm, simply cannot be exerted without a structure.

It is also true that structures can compensate, to some extent at least, for the absence of leadership, the more likely future condition in the Atlantic relationship. What should future trans-Atlantic institutions do? And what should they look like?

Common Projects or Common Institutions?

Referring to a conversation in which German Chancellor Helmut Kohl voiced concern that the two sides of the Atlantic might ultimately drift apart, House Speaker Newt Gingrich summed up the challenge in words worth repeating:

> We will drift apart unless we have projects large enough to hold us together. . . . We are not going to stay together out of nostalgia. . . . We want to do things that are large enough that they knit us together in ways that are practical, where on a daily basis thousands of Europeans and thousands of Americans wake up and say: 'Oh, this is really exciting being on the same team.' Because if we are not actively on the same team in a practical way, we will inevitably, in the long run, not be on the same team (remarks made at a conference of the Nixon Center for Peace and Freedom on March 1, 1995, in Washington, D.C., as transcribed by the Federal News Service).

Actively on the same team in a practical way—that is a useful way to define what is needed to knit the two sides of the Atlantic together again. It will apply above all in the economic field. It is here that thousands of Europeans and thousands of Americans can experience directly the advantages of a closer relationship. It is here, too, that the tensions inherent in competition need to be addressed so that they do not foster resentment against a closer new relationship among thousands of Europeans and thousands of Americans—or even against maintaining the old relationship much longer.

In recent months, a number of proposals for closer economic links have been put forward, chief among them an Atlantic Free Trade Area between North America and the European Union. There are clearly considerable obstacles on the road to such an agreement—the thorny issue of agricultural subsidies as well as the concern that a free-trade area between the richest regions in the world would undermine efforts in the World Trade Organization (WTO) to remove trade barriers worldwide. But regardless of the specifics, it is helpful to view the proposal itself as a sign of growing awareness that North America and the EU must handle their trade and financial relationships better than they have done hitherto. In the past, when the United States and Western Europe together dominated international trade, that may have been less urgent. Today, as markets have become global and major new players operate in them, trans-Atlantic laissez faire is becoming economically and politically increasingly costly.

There is a need to define common rules for investment, to agree on safety standards, and to consult on common initiatives in the WTO. The implications of the European Monetary Union for Atlantic capital markets—a matter to which Americans have given surprisingly little thought so far—should be addressed jointly in advance. Some degree of Atlantic coordination in case of major currency crises would only seem prudent, given their potentially damaging impact in both economic and political terms. While none of this would exclude a more formal Free Trade Area at some later stage, such an agreement would take decades to negotiate and implement. In the meantime, an Atlantic Economic Council should be set up to provide the procedures and the machinery to address many of these outstanding issues.

In addition to trade and finance, other practical and urgent tasks needing trans-Atlantic attention include:

Ecology. A North Atlantic Environmental Protection Forum could serve as an information exchange and coordinating body for ecological matters that rightly command growing public concern on both sides of the Atlantic.

Drugs and related crime. Since Western industrial countries offer the most lucrative markets for narcotics, close coordination in the fight against drug trafficking and organized crime would seem imperative; amazingly, relatively little coordination takes place so far. An Atlantic Standing Group for Drug Prevention could provide a network for the day-to-day exchange of information and the preparation of joint operations.

Social issues. Working groups on issues such as social welfare, health reform, or immigration could advance the trans-Atlantic debate on themes about which both American and European citizens care deeply.

Indeed, if there is the will to create a new institutional network across the Atlantic, there are enough issues to justify the effort. These are pressing tasks, not alibis for institution-building. Given the intense interaction between the United States and Western Europe, there are few areas in which closer cooperation would not be useful. Most important, a serious effort to address them would demonstrate to the public on both sides of the Atlantic that the relationship has lost neither relevance nor utility with the disappearance of the Soviet threat.

No Urgency Test

The brief sketch of desirable Atlantic activities deliberately suggests not only possible areas for trans-Atlantic cooperation but an organizational structure as well. Some will argue that institutions should be created only when there is a powerful demand for them; otherwise they could fail both do their job and to win public respect. If that were indeed the case, it would be better not to start down the institutional road. However, the argument is not convincing.

NATO, it is true, was imposed by the Cold War. It owed its existence to the need to extend nuclear deterrence from the United States to the Iron Curtain in Europe and the need to organize allied defense. But such an overriding pressure to form an institution is the exception, not the norm, for the creation of international organizations. Usually institutions are created not because they are a matter of life and death but because governments decide that it makes good sense to try to work together through an agreed procedure. Often it is not even possible to prove that, without an organization, the job could not be done at all or that it would necessarily be done badly, merely that governments have been convinced—in many instances by charismatic personalities like Woodrow Wilson, John Maynard Keynes, or Jean Monnet—that the job can be accomplished better with than without an institution. The rationale for institutions does not depend on their being vitally important but on their being useful. Were it otherwise, the League of Nations, the United Nations, the World Bank, the International Monetary Fund, and indeed the European Community would never have seen the light of day.

Public opinion is not averse to less than "vital" institutions. On the contrary, the very existence of an international institution is often accepted as justification for joint efforts in a particular field. Doing things together with other friendly states is generally viewed positively by publics on both sides of the Atlantic, provided that doing so does not demand more than it delivers and that it reduces rather than increases international recrimination. After all, what generated the enduring support for NATO in Atlantic nations was not just the threat from an expansionist Soviet Union but also the satisfying spectacle of sovereign, yet like-minded governments working together through a common institution.

Hence the test for new Atlantic institutions is less demanding than many, particularly in the United States, like to think. Although the strategic need to keep the United States involved in Europe may no longer be sufficient to convince a public rightly relieved by the end of the Cold War, collaboration between the United States and Europe on a range of common projects and joint efforts that cumulatively amount to such involvement, certainly would convince the public. Such efforts will not acquire the same degree of urgency as NATO did in the past; nothing will be as urgent as defense against a present danger. But there are enough pressing issues on the trans-Atlantic agenda that governments could address through agreed procedures. Even if the security link were still powerful enough to hold the two sides of the Atlantic together, these issues would require attention; now that it is no longer, these other issues have the additional bonus of demonstrating the continued vitality of the Atlantic community.

Why the Lack of Institutions?

If the United States and Europe have shared interests, if there are significant areas in which cooperation would be highly advantageous, if the strategic need to underpin the security relationship is evident, and if public opinion is not hostile—then why have governments on both sides of the Atlantic been so reluctant to establish an institutional base for a closer Atlantic connection?

The apparent exception is the Transatlantic Declaration, signed in November 1990 between the United States and the members of the European Union to "reaffirm their determination further to strengthen their partnership." Yet that declaration was never intended to fill the void that the marginalization of security issues in trans-Atlantic relations has produced. Its purpose was to establish regular consultations between the EU and the United States, not to replace or even underpin an alliance that at the time was still the central pillar of the trans-Atlantic relationship. Hence while its principles were ambitious, its institutional proposals were more than modest: all it did was to establish a schedule for consultations between various high-level representatives of the European Community and the U.S. government.

In general, these consultations seem to be appreciated by both the Brussels and the Washington bureaucracies. If they have nevertheless failed to establish a new political framework of U.S.-European relations, this is due to a number of factors. First, mere consultations rarely generate a sense of mutuality and interdependence. Second, contrary to expectations at the time, the EU did not develop the cohesion necessary for common foreign policymaking; the talks thus remain essentially a technical exercise focusing on economic rather than political matters. Finally, other institutions—like NATO or the G-7 group of leading industrial countries—initially seemed to be more appropriate for managing the overall Western relationship. In the meantime, the problems of an alliance that has lost its enemy and of a "group" that has degenerated into a media opportunity have become fully apparent.

Despite these changes, the Transatlantic Declaration is still the only European-American arrangement outside the security field. The reason for the reluctance to engage in new Atlantic institutions can be found in both European and U.S. attitudes. In Europe, the timetable and the aspirations of the European Union have had the unfortunate effect of blocking major trans-Atlantic initiatives. EU members have set themselves an ambitious agenda for the next five years: to make the Union

ready for further enlargement through the Intergovernmental Conference, to subsequently negotiate the entry of Eastern European countries,
and to establish the Monetary Union by 1999. There will be little political
energy left for initiating Atlantic institutions. In addition, EU governments
continue to discourage American initiatives by claiming routinely that
the United States' partner should be the Union rather than individual
countries long before the Union is in any position to play that role.

U.S. resistance to institutional commitments, however, is an even
greater obstacle. After all, most of the recent calls for a broader-based
Atlantic community have come from European politicians; if the U.S.
president were to launch a major initiative, Europe, despite other preoccupations, would respond positively, not least because of the widespread
European concern that the United States is drifting away from Europe.

There are probably two reasons for the American reluctance: an
anti-multilateralist mood among the political elites and a general feeling
that, as far as U.S. influence in Europe is concerned, present arrangements are, after all, quite satisfactory.

How far the anti-multilateralist mood has infected even mainstream
American opinion is exemplified by Senate Majority Leader and Republi-
can presidential candidate Robert Dole, who wrote in the Spring 1995
issue of *Foreign Policy* that "International organizations . . . will not
protect American interests. Only America can do that"(p. 36).

In Asia, the United States is supporting the new organization, the
Asia-Pacific Economic Cooperation (APEC) forum, in order to be
accepted by Asian countries as a rightful participant in their affairs. In
Europe, however, most American policymakers feel quite content to do
without any further institutional underpinning. In particular, they tend
to see in NATO, with its institutional memory of U.S. leadership, a
congenial framework that they do not wish to undermine by the establishment of other, potentially competing institutions.

Yet neither the anti-multilateralist mood nor the convenient reliance
on NATO as the main trans-Atlantic link will necessarily last. Significantly, all of the top foreign policy goals listed in the most comprehensive
recent poll of U.S. public opinion concern issues that cannot be dealt
with through unilateral U.S. action but require cooperation with other
countries: stopping the inflow of illegal drugs, 85 percent; protecting
jobs, 83 percent; preventing nuclear proliferation, 82 percent; controlling illegal immigration, 72 percent; or securing adequate supplies of
energy, 62 percent (Chicago Council on Foreign Relations, *American
Public Opinion and U.S. Foreign Policy 1995*).

Since these objectives cannot be reached unilaterally, they positively demand America's participation in international organizations.
Most of them are obvious candidates for a joint Atlantic approach. As

the Chicago Council on Foreign Relations poll states: "Americans are increasingly reluctant to shoulder the burdens of international leadership alone, but are willing to share responsibility through participation in multilateral organizations." While they may be reluctant to entrust the United Nations with these tasks (although, as the same poll shows, less reluctant than Senator Dole), the sentiment is likely to be very different in respect to partners in Europe with whom they have been closely and profitably involved for so long.

For those who oppose new institutional initiatives for fear they will undermine NATO, the poll holds little comfort. Significantly, only 41 percent of the public surveyed listed "defending our allies' security" among the "very important" foreign policy goals of the United States. And however congenial NATO may still seem to the United States today, this will be less so as the Alliance becomes Europeanized. Rather, NATO will wither unless it is visibly embedded in a wider Atlantic community.

No NATO, No EU Monopoly

The obstacles of timing, mood, and preference that currently discourage Atlantic institutional initiatives are not insurmountable. If governments are determined to underpin the trans-Atlantic relationship by broadening it, there is plenty of opportunity for doing so. Yet two qualifications, both related to NATO and the EU, will have to be kept in mind.

First, whatever new activities governments may choose, they must not be squeezed into the NATO machinery. It is true that the North Atlantic Treaty in its Article II defines NATO's brief more broadly than in purely political-military terms: "The parties will contribute to the further development of peaceful and friendly international relations by strengthening their free institutions, by bringing about a better understanding of the principles upon which these institutions are founded, and by promoting conditions of stability and well-being. They will seek to eliminate conflict in their international economic policies and will encourage economic collaboration between any or all of them."

If NATO were set up today, Article II might well become its basic text. But the Alliance and its organization has been around for almost five decades. All of NATO's expertise, procedures, traditions, notions of hierarchy, and problem-solving instincts have evolved around security and defense. They can no longer be changed without both weakening the organization's ability to do what it was set up to do and deforming whatever new responsibilities are delegated to it. Significantly, whenever NATO governments have tried to explore the potential of Article II, they have been unable to translate it into concrete cooperation. This will be even more the case today. Security and defense is only one area of trans-Atlantic cooperation, and NATO is only one, not *the*, institution of the Atlantic community.

Indeed, the more clearly NATO's monopoly is broken, the better. Today, not only Atlantic summits but also Atlantic parliamentary meetings are dominated by security issues and security types. To show that there is more to the Atlantic community than NATO, summits must begin to cover the whole range of Atlantic issues. Similarly, in the North Atlantic Assembly, a regular conference of parliamentarians from the member states, NATO matters should be only one preoccupation among many, and national parliaments should cease to nominate only dyed-in-the-wool NATOnians to the Assembly, opening it up instead to deputies concerned with domestic, social, and economic issues.

Second, just as NATO must not monopolize Atlantic relations, so the European Union must not be elevated to sole organizer of European views and exclusive counterpart to the United States in future trans-Atlantic activities. This is no criticism of the approach taken by the Transatlantic Declaration of 1990; its purpose, after all, was to establish formal consultative procedures between a European body growing into an international actor, however incomplete, and the United States. But it is a warning against building the Atlantic community primarily on a U.S.-EU basis and against seeing the solution to trans-Atlantic drift, as some do, in a formal treaty between the Union of European States and the United States of America.

Because of the enduring diversity of Europe, diversity is needed in trans-Atlantic arrangements. Perhaps one day, most of Europe will be included in the European Union, and all its members will then agree to conduct their external relations through the institutions of the EU alone. But that day is very distant, and trans-Atlantic cooperation cannot wait that long. Although the EU is the evident addressee in all trade and economic matters and (once the Monetary Union is in place) monetary issues as well, many other issues requiring Atlantic consultation and coordination are still under the total or at least partial control of national governments. Moreover, both the design and the implementation of foreign policy—even if it were progressively coordinated in the EU's Council of Ministers—will for a long time remain the preserve of national authorities.

Thus there are good practical reasons for not squeezing the European partners of the Atlantic community into an incomplete EU frame. There are strong political reasons for not doing so as well. European governments, when faced with U.S. requests for joint deliberation, often take refuge behind the supposed need to establish a European consensus first. But this is at best a device for delay and at worst a device for frustrating whatever willingness the United States may have to create additional Atlantic institutions. Making progress in trans-Atlantic relations dependent on progress in European integration would serve only to undermine the former and weaken the latter. It would not only fail to convince citizens on both sides of the Atlantic of the advantages of working together, but also turn Atlantic cooperation into a divisive issue in an already strained European Union. And it would vindicate those in the United States who prefer the freedom of unilateralism to the compromises—and benefits—of multilateralism.

Some in Europe will no doubt demand that the United States prop up European integration by making the EU its sole, or at least its main, partner in the future Atlantic community. These demands should be resisted by both the U.S. and European governments. The United States cannot bestow upon the Union more powers than the Union's members themselves delegate to it. Others may argue that Europe will unite more effectively in juxtaposition to the United States. That view was always naive, although not particularly dangerous, when the United States was still the confident leader of the Western world. Today, when the United States has lost the desire and vision to lead the West and needs the encouragement of its European partners, such a notion has become positively irresponsible with respect to European unity and Atlantic comity alike.

A Roof Over Many Houses

There should thus be not one, but many forms of trans-Atlantic institutional collaboration, with each arrangement specifically designed to suit its subject matter. They should all have two aspects in common: collaboration should generally consist of more than consultation, and some degree of coordination between the parallel Atlantic activities should be assured.

This requires a formal process of negotiation that commits bureaucracies and is visible to the public, a secretariat to assure continuity, and a decision-making body to settle outstanding issues. These ingredients contributed to the success story of NATO; had military collaboration been based on no more than consultation, the Alliance, whatever the commitments of Article V, scarcely would have held together for so long.

Only serious issues addressed in serious institutions can underpin the trans-Atlantic link. Consultations that commit no one to more than informing the others may be useful in some areas, such as health and social-security reforms, by highlighting the similarity of problems and identifying the lessons that Europeans and Americans can learn from each other's experience. But there will have to be, in addition, other fora in which trans-Atlantic nations engage in a permanent negotiation process to overcome differences.

Not one but a multitude of trans-Atlantic institutions—some merely consultative, others negotiating and decision-making bodies—should be the elements of the future Atlantic network. Yet these various institutions will also have to be bound together in a way that convinces the public, impresses the bureaucrats, and lures the politicians.

The supreme coordinating body should be an Atlantic summit of heads of governments every two years, an Atlantic Council replacing and expanding the traditional NATO summits. These summits would no longer be chaired, as NATO summits are today, by NATO's Secretary-General but by a president of the Atlantic Council, a position that would also rotate every two years. NATO would be represented at the Council along with other Atlantic bodies by their respective secretaries or coordinators.

Such an innovation would have four considerable advantages. First, it would demonstrate that NATO remains important but is no longer the sole institution for trans-Atlantic collaboration. Second, it would underline that stability and security are not just a military matter. Third, by setting deadlines, the Atlantic Summit would generate activity in the various fields of Atlantic cooperation. Fourth, by creating a two-year presidency, rotating among heads of government, politicians would be encouraged to put a personal stamp on their respective tenures, competing with their predecessors and setting standards for their successors in Atlantic initiatives.

Governments of course cannot and must not be the only promoters of the Atlantic community. If that community has lasted for so long, it was also because of the multitude of private initiatives and exchanges weaving a network of contacts between Europe and the United States. These were particularly in evidence in the early decades of the Cold War. They will now have to be renewed to create the familiarity on which common institutions thrive.

Yet governments are needed to create the institutions that can assure the Atlantic connection between Europe and the United States. If one looks at the domestic preoccupations of politicians in both Europe and the United States today, there is reason to fear that they will claim to be otherwise engaged. There was no dearth of domestic concerns in the past either, yet these did not prevent political leaders from establishing the institutions that helped to assure the peace during the Cold War and now have the potential of securing it in tomorrow's Europe.

The best chance for ensuring that the link between the two sides of the Atlantic does not wear out lies in the creation of a network of trans-Atlantic institutions, establishing an orderly process of cooperation across the board. This will not remove all the differences or avoid all the controversies, but it will channel them, reducing their divisive impact. It will not stop the trend of growing introspection in the United States as well as in Europe, but it will make it easier for governments to resist the temptation to give in to these tendencies. Such a web of institutions will help the United States and its European partners of fifty years feel their way through the fog of uncertain times without losing touch with each other. And it will keep the United States involved in Europe—the prime condition for the future success of NATO and the European Union in promoting stability on the continent.

CONCLUSION

Securing the peace won in the Cold War is not the herculean task faced by Western statesmen when the Cold War began. Rather, it involves adjusting and complementing the major structures of order—NATO and the European Union—that are the outstanding legacies of the unique half century that followed World War II.

Now normalcy has returned. But there is no cause for fashionable gloom. Then, war—even nuclear war—was, or at least was feared to be, a serious possibility. Now, the dangers are expressed in trends rather than tanks. Western Europe is prosperous, Eastern Europe and Russia are on the (admittedly rocky and uncertain) road to democracy and economic recovery. Structures of order are in place to help inhibit conflict and protect peaceful change.

This essay has focused on the ability of NATO and the European Union to remain relevant today. That is no simple task: both were created to serve us in abnormal circumstances; now they have to prove their usefulness in the changed international setting.

The conclusion is essentially this: NATO and the EU have not been overtaken by events. They remain the right structures of order for the new Europe—NATO because it brings the United States into the European equation, the European Union because no better instrument for welding neighbors into partners has yet been devised.

Yet neither institution can continue as it has. Both must adjust, and both must be complemented in order to perform the needed tasks in the changed circumstances.

NATO has to develop a strategy for projecting stability beyond its present membership that will not be limited to, but has to include new members from Eastern Europe. This is not primarily for the sake of the latter—altruism is rarely a maxim for foreign policy—but for its own sake: the North Atlantic Alliance will last only if its members are united by a common purpose. Military security, although still not negligible, can no longer provide that unifying purpose; projecting stability to the continent as a whole could.

The European Union, while expanding its membership, has to retain what has been central to its success: the unique blending of national and supranational elements in its decision-making. Otherwise enlargement of size will mean contraction of efficiency, and ultimately the loss of credibility. Since not all members are likely to agree to a reaffirmation of the Union's supranational character, those that do will have to go forward alone, clustered around France and Germany. The establishment of the Monetary Union scheduled for 1999—not the Intergovernmental Conference planned for 1996—will constitute the decisive test for the future of the EU.

But European stability cannot be secured simply by adding a few Eastern European countries to NATO and the EU. It also requires offering a place to Russia and making sure that the United States stays involved in Europe. The two institutional innovations that this book proposes refer to these two powers, now no longer dominating the continent: a NATO-Russia Forum, and a revitalized Atlantic community. Both proposals take account of the changed circumstances, and they are interconnected.

Because Russia is no longer a threat to the West but is itself part of the problem of instability, it must be drawn into the European stability framework. This cannot be done through offering it membership in NATO and the EU, since neither institution would be capable of absorbing Russia. Instead, a new institution will have to be created for this purpose: a NATO-Russia Forum for regular and thorough policy consultation and coordination.

And because Russia is no longer the common threat, the risk of erosion in the U.S.-European relationship has to be taken seriously. This is the reason for the second institutional proposal: an Atlantic community based more broadly on a whole range of joint projects and institutions, corresponding to needs and concerns on both sides of the Atlantic beyond those of security and thus instrumental for retaining America's link to Europe. Of all the requirements for a stable Europe, this link is the most important.

Those who regard the approach and proposals here offered as too ambitious should remind themselves of the much more demanding efforts that were necessary at the outset of and throughout the Cold War. The costs and sacrifices will be a fraction of those required then. Stability comes much cheaper than deterrence of a World War. It does not require the extraordinary statesmen of the past; it can do with the ordinary politicians of today. The West can afford to be less worried. It can even devote most of its energy to repairing the cracks in its own domestic structures that until recently were obscured by the sense of East-West rivalry and danger.

The West cannot, however, afford to let things slide. Muddling through is all right when the framework is in place, but that is not yet the case. On the contrary, with mere muddling through, NATO and the European Union could end up without a future, Russia without having a European perspective, and the United States without wanting one. The peace that was won in the Cold War will not necessarily then collapse, but it will be brittle, frail, and vulnerable.

It will not take much now to secure it.

ABOUT THE AUTHOR

Christoph Bertram is Diplomatic Correspondent of the German weekly, *Die Zeit*. From 1974 to 1982, he was Director of the International Institute for Strategic Studies in London. Since then, he has served on the editorial board of *Die Zeit*. For six months in 1995, while writing this study on leave from his paper, he was a Senior Associate at the Carnegie Endowment. Mr. Bertram has written widely on European and Atlantic security issues.

THE CARNEGIE ENDOWMENT FOR INTERNATIONAL PEACE

The Carnegie Endowment for International Peace was established in 1910 in Washington, D.C., with a gift from Andrew Carnegie. As a tax-exempt operating (not grant-making) foundation, the Endowment conducts programs of research, discussion, publication, and education in international affairs and U.S. foreign policy. The Endowment publishes the quarterly magazine, *Foreign Policy*.

Carnegie's senior associates—whose backgrounds include government, journalism, law, academia, and public affairs—bring to their work substantial first-hand experience in foreign policy through writing, public and media appearances, study groups, and conferences. Carnegie associates seek to invigorate and extend both expert and public discussion on a wide range of international issues, including worldwide migration, nuclear nonproliferation, regional conflicts, multilateralism, democracy-building, and the use of force. The Endowment also engages in and encourages projects designed to foster innovative contributions in international affairs.

In 1993, the Carnegie Endowment committed its resources to the establishment of a public policy research center in Moscow designed to promote intellectual collaboration among scholars and specialists in the United States, Russia, and other post-Soviet states. Together with the Endowment's associates in Washington, the center's staff of Russian and American specialists conduct programs on a broad range of major policy issues ranging from economic reform to civil-military relations. The Carnegie Moscow Center holds seminars, workshops, and study groups at which international participants from academia, government, journalism, the private sector, and nongovernmental institutions gather to exchange views. It also provides a forum for prominent international figures to present their views to informed Moscow audiences. Associates of the center also host seminars in Kiev on an equally broad set of topics.

The Endowment normally does not take institutional positions on public policy issues. It supports its activities principally from its own resources, supplemented by nongovernmental, philanthropic grants.

Carnegie Endowment for International Peace
2400 N Street, N.W.,
Washington, D.C. 20037
Tel.: (202) 862-7900
Fax: (202) 862-2610
e-mail: ceip@igc.apc.org

Carnegie Moscow Center
Mosenka Plaza
24/27 Sadovaya-Samotechnaya
103051 Moscow, Russia
Tel: (7-095) 258-5025
Fax: (7-095) 258-5020
e-mail: carnegie@glas.apc.org.

A CARNEGIE ENDOWMENT BOOK

TRACKING NUCLEAR PROLIFERATION
A GUIDE IN MAPS AND CHARTS, 1995

Leonard S. Spector and Mark McDonough with Evan S. Medeiros

Tracking Nuclear Proliferation provides specialists and the public alike with the latest available facts about the threat that Americans identify as their greatest foreign policy concern.

The nature of the nuclear proliferation danger has changed dramatically in recent years. On the positive side, more nations than ever before are renouncing nuclear arms under strict international control—in some cases shutting down secret nuclear weapons programs and even giving up complete nuclear arsenals.

On the negative side, however, a handful of states continue to challenge international norms. Some are attempting to defeat the nuclear restraints they have accepted. Others, already undeclared nuclear powers, continue to enhance their nuclear forces. Equally threatening is the prospect of an international black market in nuclear goods. With the breakup of the Soviet Union and possible political instability looming in China, this danger is more serious than ever before. The first cases of smuggled weapons-grade nuclear material have already been documented.

To keep pace with these events, *Tracking Nuclear Proliferation* provides a comprehensive, country-by-country guide to the spread of nuclear arms in

the mid-1990s. The present survey is the sixth in the Carnegie Endowment's series on proliferation prepared under the direction of Leonard S. Spector.

This 1995 assessment offers detailed information on key recent developments in a new, easy to use format featuring explanatory maps, charts describing the national nuclear programs of seventeen countries, and appendices introducing newcomers to the basics of nuclear technology and multilateral nuclear controls.

ISBN: 0-87003-066-3
Price: $12.95

For credit card orders, call Carnegie's distributor,
The Brookings Institution, toll-free at 1-800-275-1447;
in Washington, D.C., call 202-797-6258. Fax: 202-797-6004.
When ordering, please refer to code RVCC.

THE NEW TUG-OF-WAR

Congress, the Executive Branch, and National Security

Jeremy D. Rosner

Since the birth of the Republic, U.S. foreign policy has been an uneasy joint venture between the executive branch and Congress. Now that the end of the Cold War has transformed world affairs and the 1994 elections have turned Capitol Hill upside down, how is Congress's role changing? As the United States faces an array of global challenges—from ethnic conflict to proliferation to trade—is congressional assertiveness in foreign policy a post-Vietnam relic or a post-Cold War inevitability? Is Congress pushing the United States toward isolationism or simply toward more selective internationalism?

The New Tug-of-War addresses these important questions, offering one of the first examinations of the post-Cold War relationship on national security between the White House and Congress. Jeremy Rosner analyzes the sources of change in the relationship—shifting definitions of security, lingering budget deficits, an influx of new members in Congress, partisan turnover in both branches—and traces their influence through detailed case studies of the work of the two branches on aid to the former Soviet Union and multilateral peacekeeping. The study highlights the potential and pitfalls for the executive-congressional relationship in a new security era.

Jeremy D. Rosner is a Senior Associate at the Carnegie Endowment for International Peace. From 1993 to 1994, he was a Special Assistant to President Clinton, serving as Counselor and Senior Director for Legislative Affairs on the staff of the National Security Council.

"Intellectually rigorous, politically savvy, substantively solid, and clearly written, Jeremy Rosner's The New Tug-of-War untangles the unpredictable, unexpected, and complex changes in the relationship between the presidency and Congress that have been triggered by the end of the Cold War. Scholars, journalists, and policy makers should read it for its insights—and heed its recommendations for the future."

—Norman J. Ornstein, American Enterprise Institute

"Rosner provides a first-rate analysis of a very timely issue: the changing nature of executive-legislative relations in foreign affairs.."

—James M. Lindsay, University of Iowa

ISBN: 0-87003-062-0   Price: $10.95

For credit card orders, call Carnegie's distributor, The Brookings Institution, toll-free at 1-800-275-1447; in Washington, D.C., call 202-797-6258. Fax: 202-797-6004. When ordering, please refer to code RVCC.

UN PEACEKEEPING

JAPANESE AND AMERICAN PERSPECTIVES

Edited by Selig S. Harrison and Masashi Nishihara

For the past four decades, the United Nations has played a significant peacekeeping role based on the consent of the warring parties in Cyprus, the Golan Heights, the Congo, and other flashpoints of conflict. But the UN role in maintaining world order has been redefined and broadened in recent years to embrace peace enforcement

efforts with or without the consent of the antagonists, often in combination with traditional peacekeeping.

This dramatic change has provoked growing controversy both in the United States, hitherto the largest financial supporter of UN peacekeeping, and in Japan, where advocates of a larger Japanese global role are promoting expanded Japanese participation in UN peacekeeping missions.

UN Peacekeeping: Japanese and American Perspectives is the product of a research project co-sponsored by the Carnegie Endowment for International Peace in Washington and the Research Institute for Peace and Security in Tokyo. Eight American and Japanese specialists present contrasting perspectives on such issues as: (1) the criteria that should govern UN intervention in future conflicts; (2) the desirability and feasibility of combining peacekeeping and peace enforcement; (3) the limitations imposed by international law on UN intervention; (4) the record of UN intervention in key arenas of conflict, including Cambodia, where Japan has played a major role; (5) domestic attitudes toward UN peacekeeping in both countries; and the potential for Japanese-American cooperation in UN peace-making, peacekeeping, and peace enforcement.

Selig S. Harrison directs the Carnegie Endowment Program on Japan's Role in International Security Affairs. A former Northeast Asia Bureau Chief of *The Washington Post*, he is the author of five books on Asia.

Masashi Nishihara is Director, First Research Department, National Institute for Defense Studies, Tokyo, and Professor of International Relations, National Defense Academy, Yokosuka.

ISBN: 0-87003-066-3   Price: $12.95

For credit card orders, call Carnegie's distributor, The Brookings Institution, toll-free at 1-800-275-1447; in Washington, D.C., call 202-797-6258. Fax: 202-797-6004. When ordering, please refer to code RVCC.

109

A NEW CARNEGIE ENDOWMENT SERIES ON
INTERNATIONAL MIGRATION ISSUES

To contribute constructively to the policy debate on immigration in the United States and abroad—and to help deepen policymaker and public understanding of the migration and refugee situation worldwide—the International Migration Policy Program of the Carnegie Endowment for International Peace announces a new series of policy papers.

Three policy papers, listed below, are now available. Future issues focus on how the United States should select skilled immigrants; migration policy issues in Australia, Canada, Germany, and Japan; progress toward freedom of movement within the European Union; and the sources of modern conceptions of democratic citizenship.

1. MANAGING UNCERTAINTY:
Regulating Immigration Flows in Advanced Industrial Countries

Demetrios G. Papademetriou and Kimberly Hamilton identify and analyze the conceptual problems and principal issues involved in thinking about and developing contemporary immigration policy regimes. They argue that policymakers must develop immigration policies that are at once effective in dealing with changing world conditions, capable of reaping immigration's benefits, able to sustain public support, and consistent with international commitments.

ISBN 0-87003-069-8   Price: $ 5.95

2. U.S. REFUGEE POLICY:
Dilemmas and Directions

Kathleen Newland reviews four major elements of the U.S. refugee program—resettlement, temporary protection, first asylum, and emergency response—and argues that, as practiced, these do not add up to a coherent refugee *policy*. Minimizing the need for refugee protection should be the central thrust of post-Cold War U.S. refugee policy. Nonetheless, the difficulty of preventing or resolving refugee-producing conflicts means that robust U.S. leadership in providing protection is still urgently needed.

ISBN 0-87003-071-x   Price: $ 5.95

3. CONVERGING PATHS TO RESTRICTION:
French, Italian, and British Responses to Immigration

In this study, Demetrios G. Papademetriou and Kimberly Hamilton, focus on how France, Italy, and the United Kingdom are responding to the complex issues raised by immigration and asylum matters. They explore the often trial-and-error character of governmental responses to these issues, the absence of mainstream political-party leadership, and the growing disjuncture between initiatives motivated by increasingly restrictionist impulses and practical efforts to further the immigrant integration at the local level.

ISBN 0-87003-073-6   Price: $6.95

For credit card orders, call Carnegie's distributor, The Brookings Institution, toll-free at 1-800-275-1447; in Washington, D.C., call 202-797-6258. Fax: 202-797-6004. When ordering, please refer to code RVCC.